BHAGVAT GITA,
Song of God

Gospel of Perfection

Dr. Roopnarine Singh MD FRCPC

 iUniverse®

BHAGVAT GITA, SONG OF GOD
GOSPEL OF PERFECTION

iUniverse books may be ordered through booksellers or by contacting:

iUniverse
1663 Liberty Drive
Bloomington, IN 47403
www.iuniverse.com
1-800-Authors (1-800-288-4677)

Because of the dynamic nature of the Internet, any web addresses or links contained in this book may have changed since publication and may no longer be valid. The views expressed in this work are solely those of the author and do not necessarily reflect the views of the publisher, and the publisher hereby disclaims any responsibility for them.

Any people depicted in stock imagery provided by Thinkstock are models, and such images are being used for illustrative purposes only. Certain stock imagery © Thinkstock.

ISBN: 978-1-4917-7425-0 (sc)
ISBN: 978-1-4917-7424-3 (e)

Library of Congress Control Number: 2015914954

Print information available on the last page.

iUniverse rev. date: 09/09/2015

Bhagvat Gita

(inspired version)

SONG OF GOD SUPREME
GOSPEL OF PERFECTION

BY

Dr. Roopnarine Singh M.D
(Doctor, patriot, teacher, writer)
Hinduroyalsociety.com

GOSPEL OF PERFECTION – BHAGVAT GITA

BY DR.ROOPNARINE SINGH MD

ISBN 978-976-8239-71-6

Gospel of Perfection

(An inspired Version of the Bhagwat Gita)

Preface to the New Gita
(by Doctor Roopnarine Singh) MD

Om Sri Ganesh Shayanamah.

This new version of the Gita came to my mind as a revelation
I have read and studied the Gita from age 13 and must have
read it scores of times completely. I was told by my Guruji
Swami Purnananda that the Gita was the single greatest
scripture of the world.

One fortunate day while reading the Gita at the 3rd verse of
the 7th Chapter viz

Manukshyanam Sahastreshu

Kashit Yatati Sidhayaye

Yatatamapi Sidhanamam

Kashit a mam vetti tatvatah

Out of thousands and thousands of men hardly anyone is
seeking perfection.

And of those seeking perfection,

Hardly anyone knows me as I am

Like the sun when it appears, removes

All the darkness that is present, and shows things as they really are, so too this mighty verse of the Bhagwat Gita came like a revelation to me. The whole meaning of the Gita then revealed to me with lightening speed, and I could understand, that the great single message of Lord Krishna was for each person, his mortal duty, first, is to become perfect as God Almighty is perfect.

And I could see that all the Chapters and verses were beckoning mankind and all beings to seek this final goal of perfection –

Perfection in discipline,

Perfection in duty,

Perfection in knowledge, and perfection in devotion to God Supreme, One God the embodiment of Perfect love.

The word Bhakti became not only the process of devotion, but the culmination of the whole biological and Spiritual process to develop PARAA BHAKTI, SUPREME LOVE

Unconditional, Unselfish, Universal Love – the Nature of God Supreme Himself.

All the process of yoga, all the pathways of yoga – discipline, duty, knowledge, practice, constant devotion, detachment, concentration, and God absorption, was to realize this pure, immaculate Nature of God Supreme – in the state of Samadhi.

The epithets of

Mahabaho – mighty armed

Savyasachin– expert at the arrow

Dhananjaya – expert at creating wealth

Parantapa – greatest of the Bharatas

Madhusadana – killer of the great demon Madhu

Achyuta – Infallible God

Purushotama – greatest of all persons.

These expressions and appellations are all synonymous with the concept of perfection.

Dr Roopnarine Singh, MD (Cardiology)

To provide a short and sufficient biography of Dr Roopnarine Singh would be too difficult a task. And so I beg for your forgiveness for unintentionally missing out on some of the many feats of this outstanding man. First and foremost, Dr Singh is a devoted husband, mentor, and dedicated servant of the public. It is without a doubt that these virtues and attributes were imbibed in Dr Singh from his deep roots in this Hindu faith. From a young lad in Trinidad to a successful cardiologist in Montreal, Dr Singh has enjoyed nothing but success as his 'mantra' in life has and always will be the pursuit of excellence in every aspect of life. Now, at the age of 75, it is perhaps fair for Dr Singh to look back at his vast list of accomplishments, none of which would be possible without the love, support, and devotion of his wife Liz.

It is perhaps an understatement to say the Dr Singh is a man of faith. He is not only the author of New Gita but also the spearheading force behind the Krishna Leela in Montreal, Toronto, Trinidad and West Indies eleven times. Countless Hindu children from the Montreal community can vividly recall "Singh Uncle" (as he is affectionately known) and how his efforts helped them to gain the valuable samskaras of Hinduism. To speak a little bit about Dr. Singh's impressive work. New Gita, he has the unique talent to be able to explain the profound philosophical and scientific gems of The Gita in a simple and succinct fashion. Dr Singh and the source of his inspiration, Liz, have hosted us all at their home for countless satsangs. One could never leave their home without having the desire to come back for the next spiritual gathering. Their combined love, devotion and hospitality towards their friends and fellow devotees are exemplary and second to none. Dr Singh has founded and runs the ROYAL HINDU SOCIETY OF RAMA AND KRISHNA. As Dr Singh's record shows, he's an institution builder par excellence.

Mr. Canada is a name that will always be exclusively reserved for this outstanding patriot. Dr Singh was the brave Canadian patriot who started the Canada Day Parade in Montreal. He has organized and conducted the parade for more than two generations with annual crowds of 100,000. Dr Singh is the author of a fabulous book entitled Canada, the greatest Nation of 21st century, which was published in English and French (1993). For his great love of Canada, he was honoured in 1993 with the Citation for Citizenship by the Government of Canada. It is no wonder that he is known as Mr. Canada to the patriots of this wonderful land.

To conclude, I would like to reiterate once more that Dr. Singh exemplifies the teaching of the tireless pursuit of excellence. His unmatched track record as a husband, cardiologist, Hindu devotee, and patriot speaks for itself. My wife, Urmila and I along with our children, Archana, Ratna, Meena, and Abhaya, would like to take this opportunity to covey our warmest wishes to Dr. Singh on the auspicious occasion of Dr. Singh's 75th birthday.

May God bless the Singh family with continued happiness and the strength to further contribute to the benefit of society.

Warmest regards,

Dr Lakshmi Shanker Dube

Professor of Mathematics

Concordia University

Canada

There and then, I decided to create a new version of the Bhagwat Gita, utilising the original Sanskrit to find meaning to this new vision of the Gita. Hence I decided to call it the GOSPEL OF PERFECTION, where the word Gospel means — absolute, real truth.

I wrote in verse form, because the Gita, is exquisite Poetry.

Bibliography

1. The Gita of Annie Basant, President of the Theosophical Society, was my 1ˢᵗ Gita. It's still in my possession today.

2. Shrimad Bhagwat Gita by Doctor

   Guru Irasama Gohse of Govindaram Religious trust.

3. Shrimad Bhagwat Gita – by Swami Ramsulchdasi

4. Bhagwat Gita by Doctor Sarvapelli Radhakrishnan

5. The Bhagwat Gita as it is by Swami Prabhupada of ISKCON

6. The Mahabharata by Kisari Mohan Ganguli (Munshiram Publishers)

7. The Sanskrit English Dictionary by Monier Williams (1899)

APOLOGY AND ACKNOWLEDGEMENT

I have gained greatly form the Study of Gita in numerous references, lectures, seminars, but the greatest teacher is, I find the submissive and enlightened heart, the seat of all wisdom and knowledge of God Supreme and His creation. (Paramatma)

If there are any faults omissions or errors I apologize to God Supreme and all the great savants and Acharayas before.

JAI SHRI KRISHNA! JAI SRI RAMA.

Notes – Gita on Internet. The entire Bhagwat Gita (seven hundred and one verses) and other essays and the play KRISHNA LEELA can be found @hinduroyalsociety.com. It is Free

Go to google and click on Bhagwat Gita.

Dr. Roopnarine Singh MD FRCPC

NAMASTE, SITA RAM, JAI KRISHNA, VANDE

Signed: Roopnarine Singh MD

(BSc., –Hons. M.D.C.M (Mc Gill)

CSPQ (Certified Specialist in Cardiology)

Date: 12th October, 2011.

INTRODUCTION
TO THE BHAGWAT GITA

SONG OF GOD SUPREME
GOSPEL OF PERFECTION

Full Text of the Bhagwat Gita

@ hinduroyalsociety.com

Dr. Roopnarine Singh: MD

Author of New Gita

There is a no book, no literature, no scripture, no doctrine, no faith, no scientific treatise, no personally practical and realizable formula, for perfection, for happiness, peace nobility, greatness, wisdom and opulence, as the Glorious Bhagwat Gita, Song of God Supreme.

This Bhagwat Gita speaks of the Empire of God Supreme, unborn, perpetual, eternal, ancient, self conscious, self sufficient, self generating, independent, infallible and inexhaustible. And the Lord of this empire as pure Spirit, without figure, face, form material substance, the Supreme Brahaman, all pervading, omniscient, omnipresent, omnipotent. But the Lord, as Saguna Brahman, is the Supreme Person, the most beautiful, the most powerful, the most learned and wise, the richest most famous and independent Person, Purushotama. He is the best and noblest of beings, birthless, deathless changeless. No one is like unto Him, no one greater that He. He is self sufficient, self satisfied, self happy. He is satchitananand, absolute, eternal consciousness and awareness, absolute bliss, knowledge, information and wisdom. He is the most independent of beings. He needs no help, no sacrifice, no flesh, no blood, no human or animal sacrifice. He covets no land, no kingdom, no power. He is not partial to anyone, all are equal before his grace and Majesty. He is not worried, jealous, fearful, wrathful, forgetful, capricious, vengeful or desirous of any result, material spiritual of other worldly.

In one word He is LOVE – pure and perfect- unconditional, unselfish universal love.

Those who find this love can know Him, as He is, for He is the very essence of our being, the source, sustenance, origin, foundation and consciousness, of our divine spiritual nature. Everyone has access to Him. No one is excluded. He is our divine Father, divine Mother, divine Lord and Master. He is the ultimate Truth, ultimate Knowledge and Wisdom, Ultimate refuge, eternal witness, eternal Absolute Reality.

OM PEACE PEACE PEACE. OM SHANTI SHANTI SHANTI

The Bhagwat Gita is the Fountain of this Empire and the Lord, one God of Excellence and Virtue and immortality, and all beings can come and drink at this fountain and find the ultimate happiness, peace, contentment joy, bliss and exhilaration beyond imagination, beyond dreams beyond speed or experience.

Lord Krishna, God Supreme Himself, in the Song of God, Gospel of Perfection speaks like no authority before, in perfect, poetic rhythmic Sanskrit, giving to us a panoramic view of all existence, all laws, all worlds all pathways and the royal road to enlightenment, as distinguished from darkness. By light we enter into divine consciousness, one with God, By darkness, we are doomed to repeated experience in material existence of, birth death, old age, sickness and sorrow. We can choose the Path of Light today, as the great warrior Arjuna did, to victory, opulence, extraordinary power and righteousness. This is our eternal destiny. We are the children of Light, Truth Accomplishment, Power, Beauty, Harmony, Happiness and Righteousness.

The choice is ours to be a not to be, perfect, peaceful, blissful in divine consciousness, or wallow in the quagmire and swamps of selfish, self serving, self interest love, striking our heads against the spikes of material pursuits, fleeting material happiness, toiling night and day with recurrent sorrow, diseases, suffering, depression and hopelessness, unmindful of the Transcendence, the Beauty, the Wonder the Magnificence and Super excellence of God Supreme, dwelling in our own heart, awaiting like a bud to flower into the perfection of the Lord's grace, attraction, power, science and nobility.

This empire of existence is governed by law, physics, chemistry, biology and the laws of spirituality. The greatest law is the foundation of science, the Law of cause and effect, the law of Karma. All are subject to this law from the dynamic atom to the mighty black hole, from the lowly ant, to the giants in the animal species, from the dark demons of might, to the lofty archangels and controllers of this universe. God Supreme is the source of this law but He himself is above this law. Hence He is the Supreme Arbiter, Supreme Judge, the Supreme Witness, the Supreme Refuge. Those who have found this Lord in their heart needs no Protector, Savior, Redeemer or Refuge, for God Supreme is Perfection Himself.

Newton Scientific discovery of gravity

But the Law of Cause and Effect extends into the ethical and moral field, the law of Dharma governing the lives of higher beings, men and angels and divine incarnations, endued with reason and intellect and imagination and who can distinguish between good and evil, the path of Light and the path of Darkness.

As we sow, so shall we reap. We are the masters of our destiny, making choices at every crossroad in the high way of time. The law applies, whether we believe in it or not. Time is the representative of this law, the witness, the judge and the executioner, the bestowed of happiness and sorrow, opulence and poverty, peace and war, relation and depression, death or immortality. Like the mighty Sun the wheels of time bring into existence a multitude, of things animate, and inanimate, and then grind into dust, all existences. This process is automatic, self propelling, endless for it operates by the Energy (shakti) of the Supreme Master of the Universal God Supreme.

In this relentless march of time, the universe is born, evolves into myriads of forms, living and non living things, the appearance of the creator Brahma, the Preserver and sustainer Vishnu and the Destroyer and Recycler, Lord Shiva, the three faces of the same diamond of one God Supreme. Everything in the Universe follows the process of creation, being designed and born, matures, develops and maintained, and then gradually deteriorates and dies or is transformed or recycled. Thus the process of Creation (Brahama), Maintenance (Vishnu) and Destruction, [Lord Siva] occurs again and again.

In this process, all things in this universe appear as pairs of opposites, positive and negative, up and down, right and left, male and female, good and evil, freedom and incarceration, big and small, beautiful and ugly, demon and angel.

THE female appearances of the other 3 faces of the same diamond of God Supreme Saraswati, Lakshmi and Durga occur, representing the functional controllers of universal affairs, of one God Supreme – six faces of one Diamond.

Those who can perceive the hidden hand of God Supreme in all the phenomena of this universe, worships God Supreme, with all his heart, mind, soul and might. He is a seer, he is enlightened, he is fit for liberation. No sorrow, no regret, no lamentation, no craving- for this enlightened sage has conquered the pairs of opposites, and is fixed in divine communion, with the pure love of God Supreme, blissful wise, powerful efficient, radiating the light of communion with the highest divinity.

To know the law of KARMA and freedom from materialism is to know Dharma – the law of governance over intelligent human beings and angels endowed with reason and imagination and the facility of choice between, good and evil.

Dharma is law, ethics, morality, principles, conduct over individuals, groups, sectarian, parochial, national and international activities, and universal order and stability. By following – the path of ligh, through Dharma, a person becomes purified, in body, mind, intellect and higher consciousness enabling him or her to see truth as it is (tattvatah) and the ultimate reality of existene.

Lord Shiva in deep meditation

Dharma enables man to transcend – The pairs of opposites, to transcend, selfish, self interest love (Kama) and with the light of buddhi, the intellect will reveal the nature of soul (atma and paramatma) individual soul and the Supreme Soul. The whole process of enlightment from ignorance to wisdom is called yoga by following the light of Dharma, through the perfection of discipline, the execution of duty, and the acquirement of essential knowledge, and purification from selfish love (kama) to transcend the modes of nature, selfish goodness, passion and ignorance to acquire pure love unconditional, unselfish universe love [u-love] and the vision of God Supreme.

KAMA – selfish self interest love, love for anything other than God Supreme, is the greatest enemy of Man. Kama is like a perpetual, all pervading, mist that hides real truth and confounds the material instincts of rational beings seeking the truth. When the individual enters the path of light with this mind and intellect, to find God and truth, the grace of God Supreme, dwelling in his own heart comes to his rescue, to purify his mind and intellect of this powerful self interest, selfish, love that separates man;s material consciousness from divine consciousness. The great angels, archangels and even enlightened beings are subjected to fall from the grace of God, by this powerful self interest love called KAMA.

Man can, by employing his own talent and appropriate training and profession, achieve perfection even in this life.

This is the salient doctrine of the Bhagwat Gita and that of Lord Krishna.

The talent inherited as guna must be trained, sharpened and cultivated to perform one's duty, perfectly. The so called lowest class, the labourers, as a cleaner, can perfect his or her work with honesty, thoroughness, efficiency and pleasantness to make oneself attractive to employer, and so earn an honest and self sufficient living, in the service of one's family, community, nation and God Supreme. By his faithful service, the Lord within his heart shall, by His grace, and law, lead him to salvation, So it is also with a professional doctor. He must have native, intelligence aptitude and discipline to utilize his talent in acquiring skill, knowledge, technique, professional status and a compassionate attitude, to be a physician, and so too gain salvation through the perfection of duty, knowledge discipline and devotion to God Supreme. Society by following this divine dispensation of true caste distinction will avoid the misfits of incompetence and abuse – round pegs in square holes. The selection for duty must be advised by selfless, enlightened teachers GURUS, lecturers and government, for the smooth working of society. God is not partial to any caste distinction as repeatedly demonstrated, in the scripture, as in the case of Shavari who merited the grace of meeting Lord Rama Himself, by her devotion, duty and service, although she was of the lowest caste.

SOCIETY IS ALREADY PRACISING THIS TALENT AND MERIT TRAINING BUT DO NOT CAL IT CASTE.

Excellence in duty

The spiritual leader must be noble and selfless too. Peacefulness, self control, austerity, physical and mental purity, tranquility, honesty, he must have both phenomenal and higher spiritual intelligence (gyana) and an ability to make simple and practical the profound teachings of Dharma.

No scripture in the world in two verses alone have outlined the qualities of the executive and spiritual leader so clearly and effectively – Glory to God Supreme Lord Krishna and the Gospel of Perfection the Gita.

A perfect leader can with his resourcefulness (daksham) solve the problems of his society and with his knowledge and fearlessness combat the self serving corruption, pervasive in society and camouflaged as democracy. Contracts and kickbacks are the backbone of so called democratic government. Only a fearless determined and courageous leadership can combat the theocratic establishment, who use God as a mule to peddle and carry their evil baggage, of barbaric self enhancing doctrine, bloody sacrifice for salvation, through blood alone, for inclusion in their organizations of primitivity and darkness.

Lord Krishna Himself, through His enlightened leadership of the Pandavas, in the Mahabharat war, demolished the selfish evil reign of Durjodhana – whose counterpart we see today every where in the so called civilized world.

Colin **Powell** and Norman H. Schwarzkopf

LEADERSHIP

The Bhagwat Gita is clear about leadership, whatever a great man does, others follow by. example. Exemplary leadership is the key to the success of any society.

But the Gita of Lord Krishna emphasizes the unselfish nature of those who wish to lead. Self promotion and self agrandisement are taboo in leadership. The world today scoffs at unselfish leadership but Mahatma Gandhi, and Martin Luther King, the greatest apostles of change for for freedom acted nobly and unselfishly. While the ordinary people act mainly from self interest (saktah), those who wish to lead society, must act nobly and without self interest. Honesty and integrity will flow naturally. SELF INTEREST AND SELFISHNESS AND ARROGANCE ARE LIKE POISON IN LEADERSHIP.

Lord Krishna in two Verses in the 18th chapter of the Gita, outlines the qualities is the executive leader and the spiritual leader. Concentration and implementation of this doctrine can create a quantum leap in this world of all pervading corruption and oppression.

Courage, drive, energy, ambition, determination, resourcefulness, on solving a problem, fearlessness in battle, generosity, with personal power, and ability to lead by argument, eloquence, charisma and reasonableness. These are the sterling qualities of the executive leader the King, President, Prime Minister and Military General.

The qualities of the spiritual leader are peacefulness selfcontrol, taking hardship to accomplish one's goal, austerity, internal and external purity, tranquility, simplicity in com.portment and action, phenomenal and transcendental knowledge. These are the qualities of the true gurus.

The GITA has thousand of gems of knowledge,. But let the gita verses speak for themselves in the new version.

The Bhagwat Gita starts with the preoccupation of the blind king Dhritarashita with the outcome of the war, of his evil son Dunrjodhana, against his cousins, the Pandavas, and the illustrious warrior, Arjun, the friend and disciple of Lord Supreme, Lord Krishna.

This blind King allowed his son to virtually usurp his own power, because of his personal selfish ambition, which blinded him from his duty as a leader and King of Hastinapura (Delhi)

This is the eternal predicament, to do one's duty according to Dharma and follow the path of Light, or to follow the path of darkness, in selfish, self interest love, leading to sorrow disappointment, disaster and destruction.

The last verse of Bhagwat Gita, in contrast, gives the rewards of adherence, and practice of the Gospel of Perfection.

Lord Krishna and Arjuna

Whenever there is Krishna, Lord of Yogo (Gospel of Perfection), wherever there is Arjuna, the perfect bowman, (perfection itself), there shall certainly be victory, opulence, extraordinary power, and righteousness.

This is the culmination of the path of light. All things that men seek, can be obtained by making God Supreme, the centre of one's life, and executing one's own duty with Perfection. This is the conclusion of the Bhagwat Gita – the Gospel of Perfection.

D. DR. Roopnarine Singh: MD

Author of New Gita

CHAPTER 1

Arjuna the troubled Warrior

1. The blind king Dhritatashta enquired
   'O' Sanjaya,
   What did my sons
   And the sons of Pandu do,
   On this holy land of Kurukshetra,
   After assembling their armies
   All eager to fight?

2. Sanjaya replied
   Having surveyed the military posture
   Of the army of the Pandavas,
   King Durjodhana, at that time,
   Approached, his Guru Dronacharya
   Speaking these words.

3. Please behold, this great army of
   The Pandavas, O my Guru,

In beautiful formation
Assembled perfectly
By your brilliant pupil, the Son of Drupada.

4. Behold in this army,
Great heroes, mighty archers,
Equal in expertise to Bhima and Arjuna,
Great generals, like Yuyudhana,
King Virata and the mighty King Drupada.

5. Dristaketu, Chekitana
And the mighty warrior, the King of Kashi
Powerful fighting men and heroes.
Leaders like Kuntibhoja, Purojit and Shabya.

6. See also Yudhamanyu and Utamowja,
Mighty warriors indeed,
The Son of Subhadra, and the Son of Drupada,
All experts in the skill
Of chariot war.

7. In my army, O great Brahmana,
Please listen, as I tell you,
Of the distinguished generals,
And captains of my troops,
Expert leaders in the art of war.

8. Like your distinguished self,
These are warriors always victorious,
Bhishma, Karna, Kripacharya,
Aswathama and Vikarna too,
And that son of Somadata, Bhusrisrava

9. Numerous heroes all in battle array,
Everyone willing to die for me,
Furnished with various weapons of war,
Steeped in the skill and art of combat.

10. Vast and limitless is our military might,
With general Bhishma as our commander.
Compared to the Pandavas,
We have no match,
Even with warrior Bhima, as their protector.

11. Every man must support Bhishma,
Maintaining their position
In the battle array,
At strategic locations,
On every battalion

12. Then the great grandsire, Bhishma,
Valiant commander of the army,
Blew his powerful conchshell,
Resounding like the roar of a lion,
And giving joy to King

Durjodhan.

13. Sounds of trumpets drums,
And bugles,
Conchs and horns all filled the air,
Making a grand uproarious noise.

14. Then seated on a chariot drawn by four white horses,
Lord Krishna blew his divine
Conchshell, the Pancajanya.
So too, did his disciple Arjuna, with his Devadatta.

15. And, the mighty Bhim,
Warrior of tremendous strength,
Blew his conchshell called Paundrum.

16. King Yudhisthire then blew his Anantvijaya,
Nakula his Sughosha,
And Sahadeo his manipuspaka.

17. The King of Kashi, a great bowman,
The valiant Sikhandin, son of Drupada,
Dristadyumma and Virata,
Blew their conchshells respectively.

18. So too, did Satyaki, Drupada
Followed by the sons of Drupada,
And the host of other warriors.

Including Abhimanu,
The valiant son of Arjuna.

19. The terrible din of various conchells was tremendous.
Vibrating with power,
Both in the earth and atmosphere,
Thus striking terror unto,
The hearts of the sons of Dhritarashta.

20 Then Arjuna, son of Pandu,
   My King, Seated on his chariot, his standard,
Bearing the figure of Hanuman,
Looked at his cousins, the sons of Dhritarastha.

21. He was about ready to release his arrows,
When he thus addressed his friend,
Krishna, Lord of the senses.

22. O' Infallible One,
Please station my chariot between the two armies,
So that I may see all those
Warriors eager to fight,
And in battle formation,
And whom I must engage in battle.

23. Please Krishna,
Let me see those warriors,
The dear friends of Durjodhana,.

The embodiment of evil,
This wicked son of Dhritarastha.

24. Sanjay then spoke.
Then Lord Krishna, O Bharata
Heeding the call of his friend Arjuna,
Drove the most excellent chariot.
Right unto the centre of the two armies.

25. In the presence, of all the great leaders of the hosts
Bhishma, Drona included,
Lord Krishna said
"See for yourself, my friend, Arjuna,
All the flanks of the Kuru clan,.
Assembled for battle.

26. Here, amidst the two great armies,
Arjuna could see his relatives,
Grandfathers, uncles, friends,
Brothers, sons and grandsons,
His father-in-law, teachers,
And all who were faithful to his cause.

27. Viewing his close relatives and kinsmen
Arjuna was filled with the highest compassion,
And stricken by a great lamenting depression,.
He spoke thus to Lord Krishna.

28. My dear Krishna, my limbs fail me.
I'm shaking like a leaf,
And my mouth is parched,
With dryness,
To behold, here now, all
My dear family,
     Ready, to fight and die in this battle.

29. My body is on fire,
Every hair in my pores is standing up.
My frame is quivering,
And my bow slips from my hand.

30. O great destroyer of the Kesi demon,
My mind is reeling,
I can hardly stand up,
My memory fails me,
And I see only disaster.

31. My dear Krishna
I seek no victory, nor do I covet
Any kingdom,
Nor crave any happiness.
To kill my own family
Seems futile to me, indeed.

32. O Govind!
Of what use are kingdoms, happiness

Or life itself,
When those for whom we seek these goals
Are now making war amongst themselves?

33. See them, our teachers, fathers,
Brothers, sons, grandfathers,
Uncles, fathers-in-law, grandsons
All ready to die in battle!

34. O killer of the Madhu demon,
Why should I desire to slaughter them
    Even if I survive this battle?

35. O Janardana,
I will not fight my relatives,
Even if I'm offered,
The sovereignty of this planet,
Or even that of the whole universe.

36. O my Lord Krishna, O Madhava,
We cannot kill my cousins,
The sons of Dhritrashta or my Kinsmen.

37. For we shall find no happiness,
In killing these our enemies.
This will tangle us in sin, forever.

38. These our enemies
Stricken with greed,
　　See no wrong
Destroying their family and the royal dynasty.

39. Then why should we O' Janardana
Wiser than they,
Commit the same tragedy?

40. With the destruction in the royal dynasty.
The traditional family values
Will perish,
And thus with the destruction of Dharma,
Vice and sin will remain.

41. When morality is lost,
Women become degraded,
With unwanted progeny,
　　Destroying all family and community welfare.

42. O Janardana,
We know from scriptures
That hell always waits for those
Who are the destroyers,
Of family, Dharma and traditions.

43. Aren't we ourselves, my Lord,
Driven by greed,
     For power
And happiness?
Are we about to commit
A great crime,
By killing our kinsmen?
It is indeed quite strange.

44. To me, it seems befitting, O Krishna,
To die surrendering to my cousins,
With no resistance, And abandoning my weapons.

45. Sanjay spoke thus,
Now Arjuna depressed,
And weighed down with grief,
Cast aside his bow and arrows,
Sat down on his great chariot,
Stationed between the two armies.

CHAPTER 2

Selfless action and Divine Communion

Fighting as duty of warriors

Sanjaya said

1. Now seeing Arjuna in a somber mood,
Stricken with compassion and depression,
His eyes brimming tears,
Lord Krishna, killer of the Madhu demon
Spoke these words.

2. How now O Arjuna,
In this critical hour,
Has this shameful lamentation
Taken possession of you?
It is unbecoming of an Aryan
Famed for nobility and valour,
You will find neither happiness,
Nor fame in this your attitude.

3. O scorcher of the enemies,
Do not yield to this impotence.
This is not your real self.
Abandon this mental weakness.
Stand up and fight.

4. How can I, O Krishna (killer of Madhu)
Fight against Brishma and Drona,
Venerable teachers of mine?
How can I shoot them, my lord,
Who are worthy of worship?

5. It seems to be better,
To live like a beggar,
Than to kill these teachers of mine,
Whose selfishness is apparent.
How tainted will be our own victory
How can we enjoy the spoils?

6. To kill or to be killed, which is better?
We cannot predict the victors.
Yet if our cousins,
Who stand before us, die in battle.
We may not wish to live ourselves, thereafter.

7. Now, O Lord,
I feel weak and miserable.
I'm confused about my duty.

Please, kindly, enlighten me.
Tell me what is best for me,
I surrender unto you,
Please instruct me.

8. I find no relief for my grief,
Which renders me weak and helpless.
Even if I become sovereign of
This earth,

    And the heavens above, too
I see no remedy for my condition.

9. Sanjay speaks to Dhritarashta.
Having thus spoken,
Arjuna, the master of intelligence,
And a valiant warrior,
Said to Govind (Krishna)
"I shall not fight, Lord!"
And thus became silent.

10. Then Lord Krishna, O King,
In the midst of the two armies,
With a smiling face,
Addresses his friend Arjuna
Now all stricken with grief.

11. The Blessed Lord said,
O Arjuna, you grieve now,

For those who are not worthy of grief.
The enlightened soul grieves
Neither for those living,
Nor for the dead.

12. O my friend
Never it was when,
    I or you,
Or these kings before us, cease to be
We are always existent,
And shall be so, into the future.

13. Just as this mortal body
Assumes the form of childhood,
Youth and old age,
So too, does the immortal soul
Assume another body.
Do not be fooled by this transformation.

14. O Son of Kunti
Material experience,
    Like summer and winter,
Happiness and sorrow,
Are not permanent but temporary.
We must not be disturbed.
For they are the products of sense perception.

15. He who is steady and undisturbed,
In the midst of the ups and downs
Of material life, pleasure and pain.
Such among the best of men
Are fit for immorality.

16. The wise have realized this truth
As it really is.
Unreality has no permanence.
True reality is ever existent.

17. The soul or spirit,
Which pervades this universe
Is imperishable.
No one can destroy
This immortal soul.

18. Only this body is perishable.
The immortal soul is eternal,
Indestructible and immune to destruction.
    Therefore you must fight.

19. He who thinks he can kill,
Or believes that the soul dies,
Both are steeped in ignorance.
The soul is immortal,

Imperishable and indestructible.
Such is the conclusion of the wise.

20. Never the soul was born,
Never will it ever die,
Unborn, eternal, existing forever,
Older than the universe itself,
Is this immortal soul.

21. How can a man
Who understands,
The eternal, unborn and
Imperishable nature of the spirit,
Cause anyone to be killed,
Or kill anyone himself?

22. Just as a man
Dons new clothes,
For old ones,
So too does this internal spirit,
Take on new bodies,
And discards the older ones.

23. O Partha,
Weapons cannot cut the soul,
Into pieces.
     By fire it cannot be burned.

Water cannot moisten it,
Wind cannot dry it.

24. This soul is fireproof,
Waterproof and
Immune to destruction.
It cannot be broken into pieces.
He is eternal, all
Resistant to change,
And always excellent.

25. The soul is remarkable,
His nature is inconceivable,
Beyond imagination and immutable.
Knowing this truth about the soul.
You must cast aside this grief.

26. Even if you consider this Soul
To be constantly born,
And constantly dying,
You should not grieve,
For any person. O mighty warrior.

27. Those who are born, must die,
And those who die, will live again.
You must not grieve

Over the inevitable course
Of nature.

28. Before birth, all beings exist,
But we cannot see them.
At birth they become manifest again
To our senses.
At death again, we lose sight of them,
Then why should we grieve for any creature?

29. Hardly anyone understands
    The marvelous nature of the soul,
    Or hear of it as marvelous,
    Or speak of it as marvelous.
    Yet there are those
    Who though hearing about it, still cannot understand,
    The nature of the soul.

30. Therefore this spirit soul
Dwelling in the body is
Indestructible.
It cannot be killed,
Hence there is no need to
Grieve for the embodied beings.

31. Your duty as a Kshattriya Warrior
Is paramount.
This is an opportunity to uphold Dharma.

Therefore, you must not
Hesitate to fight.

32. Fortunate, indeed, O Partha(Arjun)
Are those Kshattriya Warriors,
Who without seeking them,
Find such opportunities to fight.
Thus opening the doors to heavenly worlds.

33. Should you fail to accomplish
Your duty,
In this righteous war, and not fight,
You will be guilty of sinful conduct,
And risk your great reputation
As a warrior.

34. Above all
People will forever,
Condemn your shameful conduct.
And for an honourable man like you
This infamy will be worse
Than death.

35. The great commanders in this battle,
Who esteem your valour and
Greatness,

Will now think of you as a coward,
Afraid to fight this war

36. Your enemies will scorn and vilify you,
With many disparaging
Remarks.
And what could be more
Hurtful than that?

37. If you die doing your duty,
The gates of heaven will be open to you.
If you are victorious,
You can enjoy earthly pleasures.
So stand up and fight
Resolutely, O Son of Kunti.

38. Fight to accomplish your duty,
Indifferent to success and failure,
Victory or defeat, gain or loss.
In this unselfish pathway,
You will never commit sin.

39. So far, my dear Partha (Arjuna),
The scientific conclusion of
Sankhya philosophy (Gyana Yoga)
I have presented to you.
Now hear about (Buddhi Yoga)
The intelligent road to selfless action,

Freeing yourself from the
Bondage of materialism.

40. In this royal path of unselfish love,
One cannot fail or lose,
Advancing on this path of
Selfless action,
We become free and fearless.

41. Those who act with intelligence,
On this path of selfless action,
Have just one goal in mind.
The energy of the irresolute,
Are dissipated,
    Following Multiple directions.

42. The ignorant and unintelligent
Are captured by the flowery (material)
Promise of the Vedas,
Thinking these material pursuits
Are the best aim of life – nothing more.

43. For this, they follow the
Path of selfish love,
Recommending sacrifices,
For good birth, health, wealth
And entry to the temporary heavens.

44. Those who are attracted
To wealth and material sense enjoyment,
And selfish love,
Cannot attain the fellowship
Of God Supreme,
    In divine communion with Him.

45. The three modes of material nature
Are all about selfish love and desires.
You must transcend these pathways
O 'Arjuna,
    And act selflessly for God,
Free from worry, gain and loss,
Pleasure and pain,
The duties of material life,
    And so obtain God consciousness.

46. An enlightened being
Is beyond the Vedas.
He possesses the world's ocean of truth,
Not just the small pond of relative truth.

47. You must perform your duty
Selflessly,
Without any desire for personal gain.
Humbly act, knowing you are

Not the master,

And never ever shirk your duty.

48. Concentrate on yoga,

And do your duty

Abandoning selfish love, be indifferent to

Gain or loss, success or failure

Such equanimity of the mind is called yoga.

49. O Dhananjaya (Arjuna winner of wealth)

You must abandon self loving

Material actions,

And surrender your love and

Actions to God Supreme (Buddhi yoga)

The self loving, selfish folk,

Become miserable indeed.

50. A man acting, in the

Consciousness of God Supreme,

Rises above the state of

Fools, and evil actions.

Strive, O Arjuna, to remain

Always in this equanimity.

51. The wise ones,

Abandon selfish love and actions,

And dedicate their lives to God Supreme.

In so doing, they free themselves,

From the cycle of birth and death,
And obtain the bliss and freedom,
In God Supreme.

52. When your knowledge becomes perfect,
In God consciousness,
And you have exit the forest
Of ignorance and delusion,
You will become indifferent,
To all scriptures, science and philosophy.

53. When your spirit is no longer
Attracted to selfish love and delusions,
As delineated in the Vedas,
And you become concentrated,
In the meditation of God Supreme,
You will become self realized,
In communion with the divine will.

54. Arjuna enquired,
My Dear Krishna,
Please describe to me how,
A man in Samadhi,
    In communion with God Supreme and
The true reality,
How does he talk? How does he walk?
What is his language? What is his posture?

55. Shri Bhagwan Krishna replies,
When a man becomes purified,
From all the cravings of the heart,
That arises from material
Consciousness and selfish love,
And finds true happiness
Within himself alone,
Then he is said to be in
Divine consciousness.

56. The sage whose mind is peaceful,
Is not disturbed by the
Miseries of material life (body, mind)
Free from longing and has conquered
Fear, anger and greed,
Such a sage is of stable mind.

57. He who is detached from
Material consciousness,
Indifferent to good and evil,
In happiness or distress,
He remains the same.
Such a man is stable and focused
On the perfection of knowledge.

58. One who is in control of his mind,
Immune to the forces of desire,
Just like the tortoise,

Who withdraws his limbs at will.
Such a disciplined yogi has
Achieved perfection of knowledge

59. Initially, the controlled mind
Will still have a longing for
Material pleasures.
But after experiencing the
Bliss of divine communion,
This material taste disappears.

60. The senses are so powerful, O Arjuna
That when stimulated,
They can forcibly carry away,
The mind of even a yogi,
Experienced in the discipline of the mind.

61. One who becomes master of his
Senses,
Fixes his mind on Me, the Supreme
As his principal goal,
Such a yogi is a man
Of steady wisdom.

62. When a man's mind contemplates
Material things,
He develops an attachment to them.

From attachment arise desires.
Frustration of desire leads to anger.

63. This anger leads to delusion,
From delusion to confused memory,
From confused memory to
The loss of reason,
And from the loss of reason, to destruction.

64. One who is disciplined,
Who controls his mind and appetites,
He follows a regulated life of sadhana (discipline)
And quickly receives, the mercy of God.

65. Having achieved the mercy of God,
The yogi becomes free.
Freed from material suffering,
He experiences peace and happiness,
In communion with God Supreme.

66. One who is not in communion
With God Supreme,
Has no control over his mind and senses,
Cannot discipline himself to seek God
How then can he have peace?
And without peace
How can there be happiness?

67. When a man fixes his mind
On selfish desires
(Seeking happiness from them)
He loses all spiritual intelligence,
Just as a boat is swept
Away at sea, by a strong wind.

68. Therefore,
O mighty armed Arjuna,
The man who is
In total control of his
Mind and senses,
In considered a sage
Of stabled mind.

69. When all beings sleep,
    In the dungeons of ignorance,
The enlightened sage is awake,
In the sunshine of spiritual bliss.
The darkness and ignorance of animal life
Is the night for the liberated sage.

70. As various streams enter
Into the ocean without disturbance,
So too, the yogi whose
Desires are all merged into transcendence,
Can at last, obtain true peace,

Not those who still crave for
Material happiness.

71. A man who has renounced
Material desires,
Who knows that nothing belongs to him,
Who has given up the sense of
Me and mine,
He alone can obtain peace.

72. O Arjuna,
This is the state of Samadhi, (divine union)
The final state of happiness and freedom from delusions.
Even established thus
At the time of death,
The yogi enters the Supreme,
Blessed state of divine consciousness.

CHAPTER 3

Wisdom and Action

Krishna and Arjuna

1. Arjuna said,
If you consider that perfection
In wisdom and knowledge,
Is superior to self-loving action,
Why, then, do you urge me
To fight this dirty war?

2. My intellect is baffled,
By your puzzling expressions.
Please kindly tell me,
Exactly what course
Is best for me to follow.

3. The blessed Lord said,
O, sinless one,
Two classes of spiritual disciplines
Have been in the past, described.
One is Sankhya or Gyana Yoga,
The scientific intellectual approach

To know reality.
The other is Karma Yoga
The path of selfless action and service
Rgarding God as the
    Highest goal.

4. A man cannot obtain freedom
From the result of action,
By neglecting his duty.
How can he become perfect
By renouncing all duties?

5. Really, not even for a moment,
Can man refrain from action,
Because of the inherent forces of nature.
He must engage in action, helplessly
Impelled by his own constitution.

6. He who daydreams on the
Object of desires,
But act as if he is controlling
His desires and action,
He is indeed a fool and a pretender.

7. But he who uses his mind
To practice control of his senses,
And execute his duty
Selflessly,

To serve God Supreme,
His action is on the path of perfection.

8. O Arjuna,
Do your duty
For which you are prepared,
For it is better to be active,
Than to be inactive.
You cannot refrain from actions
Even to maintain your own body.

9. Work must be dedicated selflessly to God Supreme,
As a sacrifice unto Him,
Otherwise work binds us,
To the material dimensions,
Therefore O Son of Kunti
Execute your duty perfectly for God's
Sake alone,
And you will become free.

10. Long ago, The Lord of the Universe, Brahma,
Created in the beginning,
All the hosts of men and angels,
Together with instructions for
     Sacrifice.
"This sacrifice will provide for you
Prosperity and enjoyment"

11. The angels (executors and administrators)
Pleased by sacrifice,
Will shower their blessings on you.
And so mutual prosperity
Will flourish on earth and in heaven.

12. The controllers of the universe,
Angels and archangels (devas/devis)
Govern this universe supplying all needs,
And are sustained by sacrifice.
But those who enjoy life
Without sacrifice to the devas,
Are robbers indeed.

13 The saintly people only eat
Food that is first, offered to God
In sacrifice.
But those who eat food not
Offered in sacrifice, but for sense of enjoyment only,
Commit sin indeed.

14. Life depends on food grown
(Directly or indirectly)
And food grains are produced
From rain.
Food comes because of rain

And rain results from
Sacrifices – as our duty.

15. Please note,
That dutiful action is
Described in our Vedas,
And the Vedas arose directly
From God Supreme
Therefore the Lord God always
Dwells in acts of sacrifice.

16. My dear Arjuna (son of Pritha) in this wheel of creation,
He who neglects his duty, not
Acting with life, as a sacrifice
To God
(Lives like an animal) sensual and sinful,
Though born as a human, he lives in vain.

17. He who finds joy within himself,
Remains enlightened and
Contented within his own soul,
Finds total happiness within,
Such a divine man is free from duty.

18. In this world, the self realized being
Has no obligation to duty,
Yet he engages himself in work,
But is free and not dependant,

On any other living being,
(And he works only for God Supreme)

19. Therefore, perform your duty
With unselfish love,
Working unselfishly, unconditionally
And for the universal good.
Work without material attachment leads
To the Supreme.

20. Perfection of work was attained
By King Janaka and others,
By performing their duty selflessly.
Engagement in perfect work,
Will also be an example to
The world of humanity.

21. Whatever a great man does,
Others follow his way.
Whatever rules he makes for conduct,
Men everywhere emulate him.

22. O Arjuna,
I'm the Lord of the worlds,
And there is nothing that I need to do,
Not anything that I myself need,
Yet I myself am always engaged in action

23. Because if I cease to act carefully,
All men will follow my example,
And bring ruin to these worlds.

24. For, if I do not act for the world,
There will result excessive overpopulation,
Bringing ruin to all creatures,
Destroying the peace
And order of creation.

25. The ordinary, unwise people
Act, mainly, from selfish love.
But those who wish to lead
The people rightly,
Must act selflessly, in the
Spirit of pure love.

26. The noble leader
Should not confuse the mind
Of ordinary unintelligent people,
Attached to selfish work.
But rather encourage them
To engage in noble actions.

27. All activities in the universes
Happen automatically,
    By the forces inherent in the three
Modes of material nature (goodness passion and inertia)

But the foolish steeped in selfish love,

Consider himself to be the creator of things.

28. One who is enlightened O 'Arjuna

Understands the nature of (materialistic Philosophy)

That the self loving mind,

Under the influence of the three

Qualities of nature, causes this illusions.

Hence he acts selflessly, seeking no reward

    And remains unattached.

29. The self loving and unwise people

Under the influence of the three

Modes or nature, indulge in materialistic binding actions.

But the man of perfect knowledge

Should not unduly agitate them.

In their selfish pursuits.

30. Therefore, O Arjuna,

    In divine consciousness,

Dedicate all your action to Me.

Free from selfish love,

Without seeking gain or loss.

Now boldly stand up and fight.

31. Those who faithfully and regularly,

Follow these my divine instructions,

And execute their duty,

Without equivocation,
Such devotees become free
From the binding shackles of materialism.

32. Those who out of anger envy and jealousy,
Fail to execute these injunctions of Mine.
Must be considered ignorant and foolish,
Lost to the hell of bondage and delusion.

33. Everyone follows the forces
Inherent in his own nature.
So too, does even a learned man.
What need is there for suppression?

34. All humanity indeed, all creatures,
Are subject to selfish, love and hate
For material things and pleasures.
But one should not yield to this culture
    of selfishness and attachment,
For they are obstacles
On the path of transcendence.

35. Do your duty faithfully,
According to your inherent talent and training,
Even if (at first) it is not perfect, and risky.
Attempting to do another's duty,
Even perfectly, is dangerous.

36. Arjuna asked
My dear Lord of the Vrishnis,
Why does a man commit sins?
It seems to me he, is drawn by force,
Against his own will,
    To commit acts against his conscience.

37. Then Lord Krishna replied
It is deep seated lust, cravings and desires,
That when stimulated or frustrated,
Transform into uncontrollable anger.
Know then, that this lust
Is the greatest enemy of mankind.

38. As fire is covered by smoke
And a mirror by layers of dust,
The embryo by coverings of the womb,
So, too, is real truth covered
By the sheets of desire and lust.

39. Man's pure sprit is covered.
By this ever present enemy
In the form of lust and cravings.
They are like fire
Powerful and insatiable, indeed.

40. This lust conceals itself
In the mind, the senses and the intellect.

And thus prevents the soul
From knowledge of truth.
Thus always confounding him.

41. Therefore O' Arjuna
Right away you must fight,
This evil creature in the form of lust.
By controlling your senses, heart and desires
And kill this (illusive)
Enemy of truth and emancipation.

42. The five senses are greater that the body
But the mind is superior to the senses,
The intellect is higher that the mind,
And far greater than the intellect,
Is the soul of man.

43. Therefore O' Arjuna,
Knowing the soul to be perfect intelligence
Superior to the intellect, mind and senses,
You must control your mind by reason,
And kill this powerful
Enemy in the form of lust.

CHAPTER 4

Enlightment in Perfection

Lord Krishna

The Supreme Lord Krishna said to Arjuna

1. I myself first taught
This eternal science of yoga,
To the archangel of the Sun, Vivasvan
He himself instructed it to the great law giver Manu,

2. This very ancient science was handed down
Disciple to disciple,
To the great royal seers, with its
Original meaning.
But O, Best of warriors, in course of time,
The original doctrine became polluted.

3. Because, O Arjuna, you are my
Devotee and My friend,
I reveal to you, this day, this ancient wisdom.

For you can now understand the mystery
Of this best and greatest of all sciences.

Arjuna then spoke,

4. How is it O Lord, that you,
Who were born long after Vivasvan,
Can say that you taught this yoga
To the Archangel of the Sun originally?
And how am I to understand
This mystery of your words?

5. The Supreme God Krishna replied.
In many, many births did you and I appear,
You yourself remember not these previous incarnations,
But O Arjuna, conqueror of the enemy,
I remember them, all both yours and mine.

6. Dear Arjuna,
Through I am unborn and Imperishable,
And the master of all living beings,
Yet I do appear by My own will and power,
As the Original Being in every age.

7. When ever there is confusion in righteousness,
And decay in the principles of religion,

When irreligion itself prevail,
Then I myself come forth.

8. For the protection of the good and pious,
    For the destruction of the perpetrators of evil,
For the reestablishment of the true principles of religion,
I take birth from age to age.

9. Anyone who can thus understand this divine reality,
Of my appearance and disappearance,
Will certainly enter into my eternal abode,
And with the death of this mortal body,
Never again take birth in this world.

10. Free from selfish love, fear and anger,
And fully absorbed in devotion.
Taking shelter in Me,
    Many great souls before, purified by pure
Knowledge and penance,
Have become transformed into My loving Nature and
    Being.

11. As people surrender unto Me
So, too, do I reward them.
All follow the Path of destiny, O son of Pritha
According to My Law of righteousness.

12. Those who seek material success,

Make sacrifices to the authorized,

Executive and administrative angels and controllers.

Certainly people achieve material results.

By serving these controllers of this universe.

13. The four social castes are natural divisions,

Created by Me according to talent and training and profession.

The inheritance of talent is a function of my laws,

I am aloof, and eternally impartial to all.

14. I am not affected by any action,

No do I seek the rewards of work.

Those who understand this divine principle

Can remain free from the bondage of action.

15. Just as the ancient sages,

Acting with such divine knowledge,

Achieved liberation,

So, too, must you do your duty

Acting without selfish love.

16. What is action and what is inaction?

On this mystery, even the enlightened are baffled.

I shall explain to you what action is,

And with this knowledge, you will avoid all misfortune

17. The mystery of Action is difficult to comprehend.

Hence it's necessary to understand this.

The nature of action, inaction and forbidden action.

Must be clearly comprehended

    to know the truth.

18. Those who can see inaction in action

And action in inaction, they are wise.

Such a person possesses divine insight,

Though apparently, engaged in all kinds of action.

19. The real pundit (wise one) is one,

Whose every act is free,

From selfish love and sensual enjoyments.

The sages declare such a man

    to have his selfishness devoured,

by the fire of transcendental knowledge.

20. Having renounced selfish pursuits,

Always satisfied and detached,

He preserves himself from the reaction

    of selfish love.

Though apparently engaged in

Manifold activities.

21. The enlightened man, having renounced

The craving for self loving activities,

And losing all sense of proprietorship in this life,

Acts for himself only to keep body and soul together,
Such a man is not affected by sin.

22. The man who is satisfied with the result of
His own dutiful work,
Unaffected by the fluctuations in natural life,
Free from envy, serene, and indifferent
To success or failure.
Such a man, though active is, always free.

23. A man who is not attached
To material self love,
And is steeped in transcendental knowledge,
Acting only for the sake of the Supreme,
Eventually enters the Kingdom of God.

24. A man whose activities are divinely inspired.
Is certain to achieve liberation in the Supreme
For him all the rituals of sacrifice,
Fire, water, butter, soul and Supersoul
Are all spiritualized in the Divine Consciousness.

25. Some mystics purify themselves
by offering sacrifices to the higher
order of divine beings,
while others sacrifice only

into the fire of absolute (Impersonal
Sprit of God).

26. Focused on attaining the Supreme by self restraint,
Some pour the urgings of the senses
Into the fire of sacrifice,
Sound, hearing and sensual goals,
Are all utilized in the Holy Fire of Self Sacrifice.

27. In the quest for perfection by the light of wisdom.
Some sacrifice all sensual and
material pursuits.
Others the life breath, by Pranayama
Controlling thus, the mind striving for yoga.

28. Sacrifice of possession in the path of perfection,
Sacrifice by austerities and severe vows,
Sacrifice by following the system of yoga,
Sacrifice in the pursuit of
Transcendental Knowledge.

29. The control of inhalation and exhalation,
cessation of breathing in the
process of yoga,
remaining in trance in the perfection of this process.,
Pranayama itself, sustains the yogi.

30. All these yogis can understand
The purpose of sacrifice,
And perfecting such practices,
Become free from sin.
They can now taste the sweet nectar
Of divine sacrifice,
And are ready to approach
God Supreme.

31. Sacrifice O Arjuna,
Is the Key to real happiness,
Whether on this planet,
In life here or elsewhere,
Without sacrifice, there's no happiness.

32. These sacrifices already described
Are found in the Vedic scriptures
These sacrifices are forms of
Work and duty
Knowing all, you
Can become free.

33. My dear Arjuna,
The Sacrifice of knowledge is greater,
Than the sacrifice of wealth.
Indeed, unselfish action as sacrifice,
Results in divine enlightenment.

34. To find the truth, one must seek,

An enlightened knower of the Truth (Guru)

Offering service with humility and inquiry.

The Guru can teach you all wisdom

    For he has directly perceived the Truth.

35. And O Arjuna, when you know the truth,

You will never again be in doubt,

For you will see that all beings

Are in Me,

And I am, their Supreme Master.

36. Even if you were the greatest sinner,

Once you have entered the ship

Of enlightenment,

You will thus cross the ocean

Of material hell,

Full of the sorrows and selfish consciousness.

37. Just as firewood is transformed into ashes,

By the power of the blazing fire,

So, too, does the fire of Truth,

Destroy the sinful results of selfish work.

38. There is nothing in this world

As pure and beautiful as,

Divine knowledge.

This is the fruit of the pursuit of the truth,

And once having attained it, in due course,
The yogi enjoys happiness within his own self.

39. The faithful devotee immersed in
Divine wisdom,
Controlling and curbing his desires
and appetites.
Quickly attains spiritual peace,
That supreme peace within, beyond understanding,

40. But the ignorant, faithless, doubting self
Who laughs and scorns the revealed Truth,
can never attain the spiritual kingdom.
To the doubting self, there can be no happiness,
In this life or beyond.

41. Hence one who has followed,
    A life of selfless love, O Arjuna,
    Whose doubts are destroyed
    by divine wisdom,
    And is always in communion
    With God Supreme,
    Such a person is free from
    The bondage of materialism.

42 You must, O Arjuna,

Destroy this doubt, arising in your heart

By the sword of Divine Truth.

Stand up and fight my friend,

Confident in the power of Yoga.

CHAPTER 5

The Perfection of Action by Knowledge and Devotion

Road to Perfection

Arjuna said:

(1) My dear Lord Krishna, you do praise

The renunciation of work,

And again recommends engagement in yoga to find the truth.

Please, now tell me what is really best for me.

The Blessed Lord replied:

(2) The renunciation of work, with engagement in selfless work,

And work done for the sake of the Supreme,

Both lead to liberation.

But work done, as devotion to God Supreme, is superior action.

(3) The man who seeks, nor craves for the rewards of work,
  O' Arjuna, is known, as a man of renunciation.
  Indeed he becomes free from all dualities.

(4) He comes free, from the bondage of materialism
  Happy in this freedom, from the bondage of work.

(5) Only the unenlightened are confused,
  By yoga as devotional service to the Supreme,
 And yoga as discipline to find the ultimate truth (sankhya).
  Those who are learned, know that the result of
  Sankhya and yoga are identical.

(6) The renunciation of the fruits of action (selfishness),
  And work done completely, as service to the Supreme
  Are one and the same.
  Those who perceive this truth know true reality.

(7) Those who control their mind and senses,
  Who have been purified, and devoted to God Supreme,
  Those who are friends of all living creatures,
   Though engaged in all kinds of activities, are free and
  commit no sin.

(8) Though acting like others with all vital functions,
  Seeing, hearing, touching, smelling eating, sleeping,
  Understands that in reality he does nothing himself.

(9) He perceives that he is spirit soul,
  Aloof from the operation of material senses,
  While engaged in speaking.
  Elimination, opening or closing the eyes,
  Giving or receiving.

(10) As the lotus leaf remains untouched,
  By the water in which it lies,
  So too does the man who surrenders all rewards to God Supreme.
  He does his duty, free from attachment and so commits no sin

(11) In order to remain pure,
Yogis renounce selfish attachment,
Utilizing body, mind and senses
In the service of God Supreme

(12) In tune with the Divine Consciousness,
Renouncing all self loving activities,
My devotee achieves the highest peace.
Those who are attached to the selfish rewards of work
Remain bound to the material sorrows.

(13) The self disciplined person,
  Renouncing all selfishness, and self loving pursuits,
  Remains peaceful and happy in this body,
  A material body of nine outlets,

In pure and detached consciousness.

He is not acting nor causes others to act.

(14) The modes of material nature

(The forces of harmony, activity and inertia)

Are the real causes of action.

The pure spirit soul, remains detached,

As master of the body,

He is neither actor, creator nor agitator.

(15) God supreme is undisturbed by man's good or bad actions.

But living beings steeped in spiritual ignorance,

Cannot perceive the Truth of the Divine.

(16) As the rising sun dissipates all darkness

And reveals all things,

So, too, does transcendental knowledge destroy

The darkness, born of ignorance.

It reveals things as they truly are.

(17) One whose consciousness is always in God,

Whose heart and mind is dedicated to the Supreme,

Becomes free from all sins,

Having taken refuge, in the Divine Being.

(18) The wise man endowed with divine perception,

Sees no essential difference,

Between a priest, a cow, an elephant, a dog or outcast.
He sees pure soul in each one of them.

(19) Those who can truly perceive this equality of all beings,
As pure soul, part and parcel of God,
Have transcended,
The threshold of birth and death.
And like unto God they are perfect,
And are situated in Brahman consciousness.

(20) One who is situated in Supreme Consciousness,
Transcends the joys and sorrows of the material mind.
His mind perfectly controlled,
Without doubt about God's existence,
Understands (reality as it is). He is in perfect yoga.

(21) The yogi in Samadhi (Super Consciousness)
Is unaffected by material joys and sorrows,
He is happy within, in union with the divine.
In this yoga, he enjoys ultimate peace, beyond imagination.

(22) The enlightened avoids those selfish material activities,
That are the wombs and tombs of joys and sorrows.
They arise out of sense perception alone.
Such enjoyment is shallow and temporary.

(23) The human being who can control the forces,
Of passion and anger, before giving up this material body,

Is a yogi, fully absorbed in the Supreme,

Can become truly and deeply happy.

(24) One who finds joy in the self within,

Is content within, finds the

Light of truth within his own heart.

He has achieved liberation, even while alive (brahmabhuta).

He has entered the Supreme state of self realization.

(25) The great holy rishis, free from sin,

Free from all doubt and duality,

And fully engaged in selfless loving service to society,

Enter into the Kingdom of God

(26) Holy men, conquering the forces of selfish love and resentment,

And overcoming the forces of the restless mind,

Quickly achieve the Supreme destination,

Communion with God Supreme.

(27) In the perfect state of samadhi (divine union)

The yogi shuts out all external influences,

Concentrates his vision between the two eyebrows,

And suspends the act of breathing.

(28) He is in, perfect control of his senses and intellect,

Having abandoned material desires, fear and anger.

He has achieved divine communion with God Supreme.

(29) Supreme Peace and Serenity
Comes to that sage, who understands that
I am the purpose of all sacrifices and austerities,
The eternal friend of all living beings,
And that I am the Lord of all created beings.
BECOMING A GREAT YOGI:

CHAPTER 6

The Perfection of Discipline

Worship as Duty

The Lord Sri Krishna said:

(1) He who performs his duty according to talent and training,
   And without seeking personal reward, is a true yogi,
   Not the one who merely renounces domestic life,
   And remains unemployed,
   O Arjuna, please note.

(2) That renunciation is yoga,
   Whose goal is union with the Supreme.
   No one becomes a yogi
   Without renouncing the craving for selfish love and things.

(3) For those who are novices in the process of yoga,
   Discrimination in action is the road to success.
   But for those who are in tune with the Supreme Consciousness,
   Cessation of material action is the resultant process.

(4) One who has curbed all his sensual desires,
   And has renounced all self loving activities,
   He seeks no personal rewards,
   And he is considered to have attained to yoga.

(5) Using the boot straps of his own mind,
   A person must indeed elevate his consciousness,
   And not let it fall into the trappings of sins,
   For the mind is both friend and foe of all mankind.

(6) The mind becomes the friend of the man,
   Who has conquered his mind.
   But the mind becomes the enemy of him
   Who fails to control his very mind.

(7) The conqueror of the mind,
   At peace with the world,
   Whether in happiness or distress, in fame or blame,
   He can easily access God Supreme, within his own self.
   He becomes indifferent to relative values.

(8) The yogi eternally happy in spiritual union with God
   Having completely curbed his appetite
      And in possession of phenomenal and transcendental knowledge.
   Becomes indifferent to the relative value of gold, stones and pebbles.

(9) More advanced in yoga, is that person,
    Who with transcendental vision,
    Sees equality in all beings
    The good and bad, the friend and foe,
    Haters and well wishers,
    Even those who are neutral.

(10) The yogi fixing his mind constantly on the Supreme,
    Should live without company, in an undisturbed secluded place,
    Constantly controlling his mind and senses,
    Knowing that all things belong to God, nothing belongs to him.

(11) To practice yoga one should resort to a holy place,
    Sit in a fixed seat, not too elevated,
    And covered with soft cloth and deerskin,
    Over a bed of kusha grass.

(12) He should thence concentrate his mind,
    And practice self control of senses and mind,
    And sitting still, thus purify his heart.

(13) Holding the upper body erect and straight,
    And gaze fixed on the tip of the nose,
    One should practice yoga,
    Undisturbed and attentive.

(14) Thus, with a calm mind, free from fear
And a life of celibacy,
One should focus his concentrated mind on Me,
Making Me the supreme object, of one's devotion.

(15) By practice of such yoga
    Regulating body, mind and senses
    The yogi reaches the Supreme destination, full of peace,
    By stopping material mental activity.

(16) No one can become a yogi O, Arjuna,
    Who eats too much, or eats too little, or nothing at all
    Who sleeps too much, sleeps too little,
    Or abstains from sleep.
    All yoga is moderation.

(17) One who is disciplined in recreation,
    Eating and drinking, sleeping and waking,
    Assiduously working to accomplish his duties,
    Reduces the sorrows of material existence.

(18) With complete discipline of mind and actions,
    And his heart freed from all material hankerings
    The yogi attains communion with God,
    And is said to attain perfection in yoga.

(19) As a lamp in a windless location,
    Is steady and without flickering,

So, too, is the mind of the yogi
Fixed in concentration on God Supreme.

(20) Achieving yoga, by stopping all material mental activities,
    The yogi feels the bliss of divine communion,
    And sees in his pure heart, the Supreme Reality,
    And enjoys this perfection.

(21) In this state of Samadhi, the yogi perceives,
    That wonderful vision of the truth,
    And feels happiness, beyond all imagination
    And above all sense perception

(22) In that trance of divine union,
One is not perturbed by the worst disturbance,
For one is thus fixed in spiritual freedom,
Above the sphere of mundane experience.

(23) Yoga must be practiced with,
Full determination and continuous application.
The yogi must renounce self love, and all its cravings.

(24) With full discipline of his mind,
He must control his desires,
Regulating all sensual material occupation.

(25) Using his intelligence and with full confidence
The yogi must gradually and in incremental steps,

Abandon all other goals in life
And fix his mind on God Supreme.

(26) The yogi must endeavor by strict discipline,
To bring the wavering and unsteady mind
To his complete control,
Whenever the elusive mind wanders away.

(27) With mind fixed in yoga on God Supreme,
The yogi experiences supreme peace
He is thus freed from all sins and selfish passions,
And becomes conscious of his oneness with the Supreme Reality

(28) In the bliss of Samadhi,
The yogi achieves the perfection of love,
And with the divine presence,
Experiences the highest state of peace and happiness

(29) The enlightened yogi by virtue of his direct experience
Of the Supreme Truth,
Sees Me equally, everywhere, in all beings and pervading
    all things.

(30) He who with perfect spiritual vision,
Sees me in all things and all things within me
Is never separated from my Divine Presence.

(31) The enlightened sage sees God Supreme
As Super Soul sealed in the heart of all beings
He worships Me as that Unity behind all existence.
Such a yogi, forever dwells with me.

(32) The yogi who from his own viewpoint,
Sees the unity and equality of all beings,
Whether they are happy or unhappy O', Arjuna,
Is considered by Me to be the perfect sage.

Arjuna then spoke thus:

(33) O Madhusudana, killer of the demon Madhu
I consider this yoga process, described by you,
Impossible to realize,
Because the restless mind, cannot be forced to
Become still and concentrated.

(34) Certainly, O Krishna, the mind is unsteady
It is strong, obstinate and always restless.
I believe it is hard to control like,
Taming the steeds of the powerful wind.

(35) The Supreme Lord Krishna, replied,
Certainly O' Mighty armed Arjuna,
The mind is restless, and difficult to control.
But by constant practice and

Renunciation of selfishness (self love),
Conquering the mind, can be accomplished.

(36) Realization of the Supreme Truth, is hard to achieve
For those unable to discipline the mind.
But success is possible, for that person
Who strives with the appropriate technique.

(37) Arjuna said,
O', my dear Krishna, what is the fate of the one
Who fails to achieve perfection in yoga,
Having deviated from this path
And who, initially, was faithful in practice?

(38) Does not a man O' Krishna,
    Shifting away from the path of God,
    Becomes destroyed like a rent cloud,
    With no stature, merit or reward?

(39) You, alone of all beings, O' Krishna,
    Can completely dispel this doubt of mine.
    Please be kind, and answer me My Lord.

(40) The Supreme Lord Krishna replies,
    The striving yogi, on the path of truth,
    Never perishes in this life
    Or the life, to come, O' Arjuna,

He who is engaged in goodness,
And devotion is never a loser.

(41) The yogi who does not achieve perfection,
    Appears again in the temporary heavens,
    Enjoying many years of happiness and long life.
    Then once more, he is born again,
    Into a family of the righteous or the wealthy.

(42) This unsuccessful yogi may also
    Be fortunate to appear in the righteous home,
    Of a family devoted to God Supreme.
    But such a birth is, indeed,
    Difficult to achieve in this material world.

(43) O' Arjuna, son of Kunti,
    In this new birth, the transcendentalist
    Quickly recapitulates his previous existence,
    And strives again for perfection in yoga.

(44) His previous life of holiness, as if by design,
    Cause him to revive his interest,
    In pursuing the divine life.
    Such an ardent student of yoga
    Surpasses all those who act,
    With selfishness, following mere rituals.

(45) However, the yogi who strives,
    By strict discipline, to reach perfection,
    Being pure and free from all sins,
    Ultimately, after many births,
    Enter into the Kingdom of God.

(46) The yogi O' Arjuna, is superior,
    To the ascetic, steeped in austerities,
    Superior to the men of intellect.
    Therefore you must become
    A yogi, my dear Arjuna.
    The yogi is considered above even great materialists.

(47) The one who is completely devoted to me
    Always conscious of Me, and with great faith
    Offers Me unconditional love,
    That yogi is the highest of all yogis.

CHAPTER 7

God as Sprit and God as the Divine Being

Lord Shiva in meditation

(1) Hear now from me, O son of Kunti
    How you can know Me as I am, and without doubt,
    By focusing your whole mind and consciousness on Me
    You shall become self realized.

(2) I shall now reveal to you,
    All knowledge, both scientific and spiritual,
    It shall explain the phenomenal world and
    Give you direct perception of the Truth.
    Thus, nothing else needs to be known.

(3) Out of thousands and thousands of men,
    Hardly anyone seeks perfection,
    And to those seeking perfection,
    Hardly anyone knows Me, as I am.

(4) Solid, liquid, electricity and heat,
   Gases, space, mind, intellect and ego
   These eight forms of My energy,
   Constitute the phenomenal world.

(5) But my dear Arjuna
   Above these eight expressions of the material world,
   There lies My superior spiritual energy,
   Which constitutes, the soul of all living creatures,
   Exploiting the potential of this phenomenal experience.

(6) Hence, I am the source of all creation,
   Both material and spiritual,
   And you must know, too,
   That by my laws they are dissolved.

(7) Nothing that exists is superior to me,
   All truths and existences rest on Me,
   Like a garland of pearls on My neck.
   I am the reality of all things.

(8) I am, O Arjuna the essential character of all things,
    I am the taste in water, and sound in air,
    The light of the sun and moon.
    I am the syllable OM, in all the Vedas,
    And the procreative energy in mankind.

(9) I am the life of all that exists,

    The original scent of soil and earth,

    The radiance energy of fire and electricity

    And the power of penance in all ascetics.

    Please understand O son of Pritha,

    That I am the eternal seed of all that exists,

    The source of intelligence in the learned and wise,

    The drive and energy of powerful men.

(10) I am the strength of the strong,

    Who have conquered greed and lust,

    I am the procreative energy in regulated married life,

    Know this, O Lord of the dynasty of Bharata.

(11) Human beings are deluded by entrancement in selfish love,

    Arising form the energies of goodness, passion and ignorance

    They cannot understand my Eternal nature.

    Who rest above the qualities (gunas) of material existence.

(12) My illusory power rests in the three modes of material nature,

    And is very difficult to transcend,

    But the devotee who surrenders his life to Me,

    Can easily cross the ocean of ignorance and materialism.

(13) The foolish and wicked, lowest in the world

    Never surrenders to me,

Deluded by my illusive energy,

They engage in atheistic, and ungodly activities.

(14) Four types of pious men O' Arjuna,

Worships Me with love,

First, those in distress and suffering,

Also the inquisitive, and the seeker of wealth,

And finally those earnestly seeking the truth.

(15) Those who are foolish, wicked

And have the nature of evil,

Do not surrender unto Me,

Do not approach Me

Nor do they worship Me.

They are under the control of My illusory maya (mystic power).

(16) Four types of devotees worship Me O' Arjuna,

Those who re in trouble,

Those who seek wealth and power,

Those who are seeking knowledge,

And the man of true wisdom.

(17) Of all these devotees the one who understands my true nature

And is fully devoted to me in unconditional love

He is indeed very dear to Me,

And I am very dear to him.

(18) Of all these great devotees
    The one who knows me as I am,
    And whose life reflect My own nature,
    He is always in communion with me,
    And in such devotion he reaches me,
    The highest goal of life.

(19) After many, many births,
    The enlightened sage
    Having known the truth,
    Surrenders to me.
    "O Vasudeva (Lord Krishna) You are everything my Lord"
    Such a sage is very difficult to find.

(20) Those who are still affected by material desires,
    And work for selfish love,
    These seek help from the executive,
    And administrative angels of heaven (devtas)
    Following the dictates of their selfish nature.

(21) The inferior devotee seeking material rewards,
    And attracted to honoring authorized angels and controllers,
    I facilitate his faith by my authority.

(22) Those self loving beings seeks favors,
    From higher administrative or executives officers of
    Universal governments and so receives particular rewards.

Know then that these rewards are authorized by me alone.

(23) Men of limited intelligence,
Seeking favors from administration of universal government,
Receive material rewards fleeting and non eternal.
These poor souls go to the planets of these superior beings,
But those who worship Me, come to Me.

(24) Foolish men, who cannot know me,
Assume that I am a simple human.
Without spiritual enlightenment,
They cannot understand
That I am the Supreme Being,
Eternal and most beautiful.

(25) I never reveal myself to everyone,
For I am concealed by my illusory energy (maya).
The foolish, materialistic being cannot understand Me,
For I am unborn and of limitless power.

(26) O' Arjuna I know thoroughly everything of
The past, present and future.
I also know the origin and future of all beings,
But no one can know me completely.

(27) O' warrior offspring of the great King Bharata,
All beings in this creation are deluded and overwhelmed,

By selfish love and resultant hate,
In this duality they remain ignorant

(28) But those beings who free themselves,
    From all sins and
    Have acted with pure love and service,
    Now and previously, they free from all delusion
    Worship me with commitment and determination,

(29) Those wise men who seek to conquer
Old age and death.
    Seek the shelter of my blessings by devotion.
    They actually know the truth about
    Selfish love and unconditional love.

(30) The wise man who understands
    That I am the God of the phenomenal world and
    Lord of all angels and archangels,
    Spiritual and phenomenal universes,
    The Lord of all blessings and rewards,
    Even at the hour of death,
    With fixed mind he can know me.

CHAPTER 8

Darkness and Light, the two Eternal Pathways

Lakshmi God of Light

Arjuna asked:

(1) O Supreme Lord, please tell me about God as Spirit (Brahman)
    About the soul of man, about the angels and archangels
    Controllers of the universe
    About self loving, material activities and the material universe.

(2) O killer of the demon Madhu (Krishna)
    Tell me about the Lord, recipient and goal of all sacrifices,
    How does he enter and pervade the body,
    How at the moment of death,
    The man of discipline, can know this Lord?

    The Supreme Lord Krishna replied:

(3) The immortal indestructible spirit in man,
    Is called the soul and

It's Nature is pure spirit,

Material bodies arise,

As a result of self loving materialistic activities,

And this action is called Karma.

(4) Physical matter is constantly in flux, ever changing,

And this universe is the cosmic expression of God Supreme.

And I am Lord of all souls (paramatma).

Eternally present in the heart of all living beings (men, animals & angels)

(5) He who at the time of death as he quits his body,

Is fully conscious of Me, remembering Me

Immediately assumes my own Nature.

Of this liberation of the soul there is no doubt.

(6) O son of Kunti, whatever a man remembers,

(Result of his main goal in life)

On quitting this body, that form of being he will assume,

This is the truth indeed.

(7) Therefore O' Arjuna you must always remember me,

Even while doing your duty as a fighter.

Dedicate your mind, intellect and heart

To me in love,

In this way, you shall certainly attain Me.

(8) He who by constant practice,

    Fixes is mind and intelligence

    On me as the Supreme Eternal God.

    Without being distracted or wavering,

    Is sure to attain Me, O' Partha

(9) To meditate on Me, one shall consider me as,

    The master of all knowledge and eternal,

    As the most ancient and original being, smaller than the smallest,

    And greater than the greatest,

    The one who sustains all life and the universe

    The Supreme God inconceivable,

    And he like unto the effulgent sun,

    Dissipates the darkness of ignorance.

(10) The yogi who at the moment of death,

    Fixes his life energy (prana),

    Between the two eyebrows and

    By the power of yoga without distraction,

    And with total love for My person,

    Certainly reaches Me the Supreme Lord.

(11) Those sages who practice celibacy,

    Study the Vedas, and chant the divine syllable OM,

    Enter into Brahman the Universal Spirit of God,

    How they do so I shall now explain.

(12) The yogi controls his mind and senses,

Closes all the doors of the mind.

And fixes his concentration on the Supreme Truth,

Directs his life energy in his head,

And thus is established in union with the absolute God.

(13) Having perfected the yogi technique,

And filled with the vibration of the chanting of OM,

Fixed upon my person in full consciousness and love,

Anyone on quitting his body thus, enters into the Kingdom of God.

(14) I am indeed O' Partha very easy to attain

For the devotee who constantly remembers me without fail,

For he is always engaged in the process of yoga striving,

For perfection to reach me

(15) Having thus attained me the great mahatmas (great souls)

Never return to this mortal world, full of sorrows.

For they have achieved the highest perfection,

The ultimate Supreme destination

(16) From the highest planet of the Creator Brahma,

And all the other lower planets,

Birth and death take place continuously.

But one who enters into my kingdom

Is never again born into this phenomenal world.

(17) A thousand cycles of billions of years (4.3 billion)
Constitute one day in the life of the creator Brahma,
Similarly one thousand such cycles
Constitute a night in earthly calculation.

(18) From the un-manifest at the origin of Brhama's day
Billions of human beings appear in the universe,
And all these are these destroyed,
As the cycle of night comes into being.

(19) By my law automatically the total sum of living creatures,
Make their appearance, and again and again they are destroyed,
Brahma's cycle of night and day O' son of Pritha is relentless.

(20) Besides these manifest and un-manifested creation,
There is a superior existence of mine,
It is eternal and the highest reality,
It is never ever subject to destruction.

(21) That Superior existence is described as not manifest,
It is the supreme and final destination.
It is also the infallible source of all existences,
When you reach that place you never return,
This perfect distination is my Supreme residence.

(22) The light and darkness are the two eternal paths
Described by the scriptures (Vedas),
When one quits this body in light

One never returns but go to God

When one quits in darkness,

One returns again to the material world.

(23) The enlightened yogi understands,

These two paths and is never mistaken.

Therefore at every moment of your life, O' Arjuna

Be fixed in devotion to me in this light of communion
with God.

The yogi who is devoted to Supreme Truth

Surpasses the merits of sacrifices, austerities, pious deeds
and charities

Finally he reaches my Supreme destination.

(24) (Of these two path that path in which

Agni the fire God and angels presiding over daylight,

The bright fortnight and the six months,

Of the northward travel of the sun,

If one proceed, along this pathway,

Who have followed the path of Brahman,

Being led by the above angels,

Finally reach God Supreme.

(25) The next path is that where there are angels,

Who preside over darkness,

Smoke, night and the dark fortnight

And the six months of the southern part of the sun,

That yogi who is not perfect,

Taking this path after death,

Is led by the above angels,

And reaching the splendor of the moon

He enjoys the results of his good deeds,

But must eventually return to this mortal world.

(26) Light and darkness are the two eternal paths,

O Arjuna and they are considered eternal.

Traversing the path of light,

One reaches the supreme state,

From which there is no return.

Proceeding by the path of darkness,

One returns to this mortal world,

And is subject again to birth and death.

(27) O' Arjuna knowing now the secret of

These two paths of light and darkness,

You will not be deluded,

Therefore at all times be always fixed in yoga,

Constantly fixing your mind on My Supreme divine nature.

(28) That yogi knowing this ultimate truth

Surpasses without doubt all the rewards

Enumerated in the Vedas.

The yogi is above the performance of sacrifice,

Austerities and charities,

And attains the Supreme goal of divine consciousness,

And union with My supreme nature.

CHAPTER 9

Finding God Supreme
beyond the Confines of Nature

The Blessed Lord said:

(1) Because you are pure and you are my friend,
   I will impart this most confidential secret to you,
   It is the essence of both phenomenal
   And knowledge (direct path to God) transcendental,
   Knowing such truths you shall become free.

(2) This knowledge is the king of wisdom,
   Most confidential and most pure,
   It is the highest and greatest of all sciences,
   By it reality is directly experienced,
   And everlasting joy and happiness is the result.

(3) Those who have no faith in this true religion (O chastiser
   of the enemy)
   Can never attain me in my abode.
   They return again and again to birth, suffering and death,
   In this mortal world.

(4) In my immaterial form as Supreme Spirit,
   This entire universe through all beings depend on me,
   Yet I am independent of them all.

(5) Though all creation depends on me,
   I am aloof from them all,
   By my law, all things are maintained and I am present
   everywhere,
   Yet I am the source of all creations,
   Behold my mystic power.

(6) As the great powerful restless wind blows continuously,
   Anchored in space, so too do all beings exist in me.
   Please try to visualize this phenomenon.

(7) O' Arjuna, all beings in this universe and all of nature
   After trillions of years (292 trillion) of existence,
   Enter into my being at the end of the creative cycle,
   Ana again at the beginning, they all are created again
   and again.

(8) I am the Lord of the whole cosmic universe,
   By my law and will the universe is continuously born,
   And again continuously dies automatically.

(9) O' Arjuna, victorious in making wealth,
   Although I have created this universe,
   I am independent and free.
   Nothing I have created can affect me,
   I am above all laws.

(10) By My own self O' Arjuna
   I pervade the whole universe,
   And from Me proceed all beings in this creation,
   Consisting of both living and non living things
   It is from Me, the great cause, that this universe is maintained.

(11) O son of Kunti, I am the Lord of this whole cosmic manifestation.
   All things and beings mobile or stationery work by my laws.
   Under my supervision this universe is functioning.

(12) The spirituality ignorant laugh at me, thinking that
   I am merely human,
   They do not understand my Supreme Nature
   And my sovereignty and dominance
   Over all things and all beings.

(13) By denying my sovereignty and even existence,
　　These fools become confused.
　　Their hopes for freedom, their self loving creations,
　　And philosophy of life are all destroyed,
　　They become atheists and evil minded,
　　But great enlightened souls,
　　Taking refuge under my divine protection,
　　Worship me with unconditional love, continuously,
　　For they fully understand my supreme nature.
　That I am the original Supreme God eternal and infinite,

(14) With great will and discipline,
　　They continually sing my glories,
　　Bowing down before my exalted presence,
　　These great souls offer me their adoration.

(15) Those who pursue the path of knowledge
　　Seeking me as the Supreme Truth,
　　Worship me as one without second, One God,
　　The reality behind the manifold universe,
　　And present in my mighty universal form.

(16) For I am the elements of all sacrificial devotion,
　　I am ritual, sacrifice,
　　I am the medical herb,
　　The great Vedic chants of adoration.
　　I am the butter of the fire in sacrifice.

(17) I am the father, mother and supporter of the universe,
　　Indeed, I am the great grandsire,
　　　I am the object of wisdom, the one who purifies all things,
　　I am the sacred syllable Om used in all prayers
　　And the Vedas Rig, Sama and Yajur I am.

(18) I am the great Lord, the goal of all life
　　I am the master of all things,
　　The eternal witness in the heart,
　　The resting place and refuge of all.
　　I am the friend of all beings
　　I am Alpha and Omega the beginning and the end,
　　Eternal, imperishable source of all things.

(19) I am the source of heat and energy,
　　I command the rain and drought,
　　I am the nectar of immortality,
And death personified.
　　I am eternal reality and beyond its domain, inexhaustible.

(20) Those who study the sacrificial and self loving parts of the Vedas,
　　Rig, Yagur and same Veda,
　　Seeking temporary heavenly rewards
　　Drink the soma juice of sacrifice to purify them.
　　　By such pleasing of archangels they worship me only superficially

And so reap the temporary heavenly joys in the kingdom of
Indra, Archangel of Heaven.

(21) This temporary heavenly solace comes to and end so
The unenlightened self loving being,
Must return to this world of sorrows.
Temporary happiness is their lot
For they understand the Vedas only superficially

(22) But those who seek the Supreme Truth
Fixing their mind on me, the Supreme
Worshipping me with devotion and care
I personally take care of their needs
To make them perfect.

(23) When the self loving with faith seeks
The shelter of archangels or higher controllers
Pleasing them with sacrifices, O son of Kunti
Not knowing me as the Lord of Sacrifice,
They do so with ignorance

(24) I am the Supreme Lord, goal and merit of all sacrifices,
Those who are ignorant of my Supreme position,
Must resort again to this mortal world.

(25) Those who seek and please angels and archangels,
Ancestors and the departed ghosts and fairies,
Are born among such beings,

But those who worship me in full knowledge,
Attain my supreme abode.

(26) Those who offer me worship with a fruit, a flower,
A leaf or water with unconditional love
That I will accept, for it is offered with true devotion.

(27) My dear Arjuna, whatever you do, whatever you offer,
Whatever you eat, whatever you give away,
Or whatever sacrifices, you perform,
Please do that as an offering to Me.

(28) Therefore you must renounce
Both selfish good deeds and evil action,
Both binding you to the material world.
Worship Me by making Me your Supreme goal,
Hence you will be free and come to Me.

(29) I am equally disposed to all beings,
Showing no enmity or partiality,
But those who worship me with selfless love,
Are always within my inner circle.

(30) Such a devotee who happens to commit a grave sin,
Must still be considered a saintly being
If he is still steeped in my loving service and devotion

(31) Such a devotee very quickly becomes righteous,
And attains everlasting peace.
Please declare, O son of Kunti
That my devotee never perishes.

(32) Those who seek the shelter of my protection and blessings,
Be they born with a lower talent in lower families,
Women merchants, servants and workers,
They all can approach directly, Me their master and maker.

(33) How much more fortunate are the righteous,
And noble royal sages and brahmans?
My devotees who in this transient miserable world,
Worship me with unconditional love.

(34) O' Arjuna, please become my devotee,
Bow down to Me and worship Me with love.
Absorbed in my loving, devotional selfless service,
You will certainly come to me.

CHAPTER 10

The limitless Glory of God Supreme

Lord Vishnu

O Mighty armed Arjuna, heed again

(1) My Supreme Instruction:
    I am teaching you this for your own welfare,
    Because you are my very dear friend.

(2) Listen, O' Arjuna
    All the great angels, archangels, controllers of this universe,
    Even enlightened sages,
    Cannot completely fathom my origin,
    For I am indeed the origin and source of
    All these great sages and personalities.

(3) Those enlightened doubtless souls who can understand,
    That I am unborn and the original first being,
    Indeed the Supreme God of all creations including heaven.
    Such a person becomes free from all sins.

(4) The great qualities found in life are all created by Me
   Intellect, intelligence freedom from delusion and ignorance
      Truth, forgiveness, peace and discipline
      Happiness and sorrow, birth and death
      Fear and fearlessness too.

(5) Non violence, equanimity, silence and penance
      Caring and charity, honor and dishonor,
      All these qualities of men and angels,
      I have ordained by My own will.

(6) The four great sages (Sanaka, Sanandan, Sanatan and Sanatkumar
      And following them the seven great rishis
      All progenitors of mankind are creations of
      My own mind and intelligence
      All life evolve from them.

(7) He who understands my mystic power,
      And knows me as I am,
      Worships me with all their heart and soul
      Of this there is no doubt.

(8) I am the source of the whole creation,
      And I pervade, the entire universe
      The enlightened, who understand my glories
      Worship me with unconditional love,

(9) Their minds are fixed on Me,
   They consider me their goal in life,
   They discuss my glories amongst themselves.
   Thus, they experience immense joy and deep satisfaction.

(10) Those who are always engaged in my contemplation
   With loving devotional service,
   I personally provide the instruction and intelligence,
   So that they can come to Me

(11) To show them my unique mercy,
   I dwelling in their own heart,.
   Destroy with the shining light of wisdom,
   The spiritual darkness born of ignorance.

Arjuna declares:

(12) You, O Lord, are the Supreme, Transcendent God,
   The best and most beautiful person,
   The Sustainer of all things, the Supreme Purity and the
   Eternal, unborn divine being.

(13) All the great sages and great rishis (enlightened ones) and
   Narada the great sage,
   Also Asita, Devala and Vyasa
   Proclaim your glory and sovereignty,
   And you yourself now declare this to me.

(14) All this that you have declared to me are true O Lord,
  Neither the angels or archangels or the great demons
  Can understand thy true Self, O God Supreme.

(15) Only you yourself, by your own self,
  Know clearly your own powers,
  You are indeed God of all deities,
  Lord of this Supreme, Creator and protector of this universe.

(16) My dear Lord Krishna,
  Please kindly reveal to me without exception,
  Your own wonderful powers and opulences,
  By which you pervade this whole universe,
  And in which you exist eternally.

(17) How can I contemplate you always
  O Supreme Mystic, Lord of all opulences?
  Please tell me in some detail O God,
  How you are to be remembered by Me, how
  I should meditate on you.

(18) O destroyer or atheistic beings,
  Please describe to Me again
  The source of your Mighty Power, and excellence
  For I will never become bored,
  Listening to your sweet discourse.

(19) The Supreme Lord said,

My opulence and powers are infinite, O' Arjuna.

But I shall indeed describe to you

The principal manifestation of

My divine wonder and glory.

(20) I am the Supreme Soul, O' Arjuna

Conqueror of darkness,

I am seated in the heart of all beings,

I am the origin, the middle and end of all beings.

(21) Of the Adityas, Lords of Light,

I am Vishnu, of Majestic Radiance.

I am the Sun.

Of the Lords of Space I am Marici.

And of nightly Brilliance, I am the moon.

(22) Of all Vedas, I am the (divine hyms).

Of musical prayers, the Gayatri

Of celestial archangels I am King Indra, the lord of heaven.

Of all senses, I am the mind

And in living creatures

I am the vital force.

(23) Of eleven rudras, executors of the universe,

I am Lord Shiva, I am Kuvera Lord of the celestial beings,

Of the controllers of the universe, I am fire and electricity,
And of all great mountains I am a Meru

(24) Of all celestial clergy, I am the Lord Brihaspati, great
guru of angels.
I am the greatest general Skanda son of Lord Shiva.
I am also the great ocean, King of all reservoirs.

(25) I am Bhrigu of the Maharishis (enlightened beings)
I am OM the sound of the Absolute truth of sacrifices,
I am the chanting of the Holy name of God,
And of most resistant things the Himalaya mountains.

(26) Of all great trees I am the opulent Banyan tree,
Of all celestial angels, I am the devotee Narada.
Of heavenly singers I am Chitrarath.
And of all perfect beings, I am Lord Kapila.

(27) Of horses I am Ucchaivastrava,
At the beginning of creation
Arising from the great ocean,
When divine beings sought immortality.
Of great elephants I am Airavata,
And among humans I am the King.

(28) I am the lighting thunderbolt of all weapons,
I am surabhi cows, productive of milk,
Of Procreators I am the Lord of Love, Cupid.

And of great serpents I am Vasuki.

(29) I am the thousand headed divine serpent, Ananta, called Sesa,

I am the lord of Sea and oceans, Varuna.

I am Aryama, King of departed souls,

And of regulators and judges, Death Himself (Yama).

(30) I am Prahlada, great devotee, though born among demons,

I am Time that destroys everything

I am the Lion, King of Beasts,

And I am Garuda, carrier bird of Lord Vishnu.

(31) I am the wind, of all things that purify.

Of great warriors

I am Rama conqueror of Ravana.

I am Makar, great shark of the seas.

And among holy rivers the Ganges.

(32) I am the womb and tomb of the universe,

And also when it is at its peak.

I am the science of finding God.

The greatest of all learning,

And of those experts in speech,

I am persuasion.

(33) Of the alphabet I am the letter A
   Of long words I am the compound word.
   I am eternal time.
   I am Bramha, the Creator who continuously sees all things

(34) I am death, the harvester of all creations,
   I am the womb of which all things evolve,.
   Of gentle qualities, I am fame, fortune,
   Speech and memory.
   Intellect, determination and forgiveness.

(35) I am the sweet, midnight hymns,
   Of the Sam Veda
   Of beautiful verses, the Gayatri Mantra
   Of months I am cool November, December
   And of the four seasons,
   Radiant spring.

(36) I am the gambling dice of the cheaters,
   I am the splendor of all wonderful things.
   I am victory, I am resolution in duty,
   I am the power in powerful beings.

(37) I am Krishna, Lord of the Vrishnis
   And of your own dynasty, I am your self Arjuna.
   I am Vyasdeva, of all sages.

And of great intellectual poets,
    I am Kavi Ushaan.

(38) Of the dispensers of justice,
    I am the royal septre.
  Of those who seek victory I am the righteous government.
    Of confidentiality, I am silence.
    And of all knowledge I am supreme wisdom.

(39) Whatever exist in this universe, O' Arjuna,
    Know me to be its source,
    There is nothing in the wide world,
    Mobile or stationary, that can exist without Mc,

(40) O' Arjuna, there is no end to My divine glories.
    Whatever, I have described, is only illustrative,
    Of My immeasurable Opulence.

(41) Whatever is beautiful, noble, great and opulent
  Divine, know that to arise from only a spark of My Glory
    But why do you seek such details,
    O' Arjuna?
    Behold, with only one fragment of my own self,
    I create and pervade this whole universe.

CHAPTER 11

The Universal Divine Vision

Universal form of God Supreme

(1) Out of thy mercy O Lord,

    You have revealed to me,

    The secret and confidential information,

    Necessary to attain salvation.

    With this education, my uncertainty and illusion,

    Have all disappeared.

(2) O Lotus eyed, Lord of imperishable glories,

    From you I have heard how each being,

    Enters and leaves this universe.

    All these things and detail, you have revealed.

(3) But now, I wish to see,

    Your masterful Supreme form,

    O lord of all souls, highest of all persons,

    I wish to see that divine sovereign personality,

    Though I can see your present form.

(4) If you O Lord believe
   That I a simple mortal,
   Can behold thy supreme mystic form,
   Then please reveal it to me, O Lord of all yogis.

(5) The Supreme lord replied,
   Behold, O' Partha my universal form,
   Thousands and thousands of divine beings
   In beautiful colourful variety,
   Within my very own self.

(6) O hero of the dynasty of Bharata,
   Behold within me,
   The principal lords of universal government,
   Controllers, Archangels and Angels
   The Adityas, The Rudras, Ashvins and the Maruts
   You can see here, wonders never seen before.

(7) In this one body of mine,
   You can immediately, see completely,
   Everything that you wish to see,
   Or may long to see later moving or immobile,
   Everything is visible, within my universal form.

(8) But, certainly, your human eyes cannot,
   See me as I am, now

Hence, I give to you divine eyes,
To view my supreme yogic opulence.

Sanjaya then remarked:

(9) Then Lord Krishna having thus spoken, O King,
Reveal to Arjuna,
His most exalted divine form,
The most powerful mystic,
Reveals his opulences to his devotee,

(10) With many mouths and eyes,
With many dazzling, divine ornaments.
It was wonderful to behold,
With many uplifted, divine weapons!

(11) The Lord was dressed profusely,
And beautiful ornaments and garlands,
Decorated His Person.
Wonderful divine fragrances smeared His body,
His personal presence appeared,
Unlimited and reaching to infinity.

(12) If a thousand suns,
Should suddenly appear in the sky,
That dazzling splendor and light

Would resemble the majesty,
Of this universal form of God Supreme.

(13) Right in this marvelous body of the Lord
One could see in unity,
The whole cosmic manifestation,
Simultaneously all in one,
But revealing multiple compositions.

(14) Then the warrior Arjuna,
In great awe and wonder,
The hairs in his body, standing on end,
Began to offer obeisances to that great,
Personality of God Supreme.
And bowing his head with folded arms
Offered his prayers.

(15) O my dear Lord,
I can now see in your body all assembled beings,
Lord Brahma the creator, on his lotus throne.
Lord Shiva the regulator of the universe,
Great sages, angels and divine serpents.

(16) With many mouths and arms,
With many stomachs and eyes
There is no end,
To this infinite form of yours, my God,

There is no end, beginning or middle
To this unlimited expansion.

(17) The blinding lights and brilliance
Like unto suns,
In such an immeasurable abundance
Makes it difficult to observe your divine weapons,
Helmets, maces and revolving discs.

(18) You are the Supreme Primal source,
And foundation of the universe.
You are the eternal refuge of all.
You are the protector and maintainer
Of the Supreme Eternal religion,
You alone I consider to be God Supreme.

(19) There is no end to thine,
Expansive manifestation,
Beginning, middle or end.
You possess infinite arms,
And I see the sun and moon as your eyes,
Fire blazes from your beautiful mouth,
And by Your own energy,
You are heating up this whole universe.,

(20) O great Lord, though you are one
And the unity behind this manifold universe,
I see that you are expanding from heaven to earth,

In all directions and all luminaries,

And all beings are trembling in your awful presence.

(21) All the angels from heaven indeed,

Enter thy being and with folded arms,

And in great awe bow down to You in prayers

The great sages and perfected beings,

Chant vedic hymns before your Majesty

(22) The great controllers, and controllers of Thy power.

The eleven forms of Lord Shiva,

The twelve Adityas, the Sadhyas, and Ashwin Kumar,

The illustrious ancestors, gandharvas

With executive and administrative functions,

Behold you in wonder

The great demons and atheists are perplexed by Thy presence.

(23) I, too am frightened by your threatened form

With many faces, arms, bodies, legs and fierce teeth.

Al the world and their rulers

Stand in fear of you.

(24) O Supreme God Vishnu,

I can no longer maintain my equilibrium and sanity.

Seeing your enormous form

Reaching the sky,

And with glowing colors everywhere,
Your great eyes and mouth make me afraid.

(25) O God of all deities, refuge of all worlds,
I am unable to stand still, seeing your terrible teeth,
And blazing face like that of death himself,
I am in terror O God.
Please have mercy on me.

(26) What wonder O Lord!
I can now see the evil sons,
Of the blind King Dhritashrashta,
Our enemies and our soldiers too,
All their heads crushed between thy terrible teeth.

(27) They and their associate allies are all being crushed,
As they enter Thy enormous mouth.

(28) As great rivers enter,
Into the billowing waves of the ocean,
So, too, do the mighty kings of this earth,
Enter Thy fiery mouth and being consumed.

(29) As moths and flies swiftly
Meet their death in fire,
So too do all creatures,
Immediately meet death in thy jaws.

(30) O Vishnu, your pervasiveness in radiance,

    Is from earth to heaven.

    And you consume with your scorching rays

    The whole universe, and all its inhabitants.

(31) I bow down to you O Lord,

    Most elevated of divine beings of presentation formidable.

    I crave to know who you really are,

    And the purpose of your divine incarnation.

The Supreme God Krishna said:

(32) I am Time, harvester of worlds,

    I have come to destroy all these hosts of soldiers,

    No one of these warriors in battle array will escape death,

    You alone will survive this war.

(33) Therefore rise up O warrior,

    Expert in arrows (Savyasacchin), now fight,

    You will conquer your enemies,

    And gain great fame,

    You will win a prosperous kingdom and enjoy sovereignty,

    Just be my instrument in this great battle.

(34) The great generals Bhisma, Drona and Jayadratha and Karana.

    By my will, they are all destroyed, O friend.

Do not worry, just fight and victory is yours.

(35) Hearing the soothing and uplifting words of Krishna,
Arjuna stood up trembling,
In body and arms and still weak.
He offered with folded palms,
His supplication to God Supreme,
Uttering these words.

(36) For good reason O Lord, master of discipline,
The entire world falls in love with you,
And marvelously delights in your glories.
The evil demons scatter every where full of fright,
But perfect devotees bow down to Thy majesty.

(37) O my dear Lord
Why should everyone not adore you thus,
For you are superior,
Even to the creator Brahma,
You are Lord of Lords, and master of the Universe,
You are infinite.
You are the imperishable foundation,
Both cause and effect and the eternal Supreme being.

(38) O Lord Refugee of this world,
You re the supreme God in person
First and most Ancient Being.
You are omniscient and all

Truth rest in you.

You are transcendental to material experience,

You pervade this universe,

In unlimited expansions.

(39) You are the great forces,

Archangels of heaven,

You are the ruler of the wind,

You are the archangel of death

The Lord of the seas (Varuna)

And you are the moon (Shashi)

You are the father of all Beings,

Indeed you are the Father

Of the creator Brahma himself.

I therefore offer you my obeisances,

One thousand times,

Again and again.

(40) My respectful obeisances, to you My Lord

From every direction

From side to side, front and back,

Because you are the focus of all things,

And you pervade the whole universe

With your presence.

In you, lies unlimited power,

And infinite strength,

You are the soul of the universe

(41) O My Krishna, O My friend, O kinsman,
I have addressed you as such,
Without knowing your divine glories,
O infallible one, please forgive me,
For my foolishness, and childish love.

(42) While joking, in play or at the bedside,
    While having dinner, or in competition,
I have dishonored you My Lord,
     Even in the presence of friends,
     Or while alone I have offended Thee,
     Please excuse my sins, O great Lord.

(43) O' Lord, you are the father of this universe,
Of whatever is moving or stationery,
    You are the Spiritual glorious master of all truth,
    How could anyone be superior to you?
    Your infinite power surpasses all!

(44) You must be worshipped as God Supreme (one without
    a second)
    I kneel before you to offer my respects.
    As a son to his father, as friend to a great friend
    As a beloved devotee to his beloved Lord,
    I implore you to tolerate my sins.

(45) O embodiment of Universal Power, may I now see you

    With your four armed form (with crown, great club and
    rotating saw like weapon (chakra),

    Vibrating conch and lotus flower,

    I crave to see you in this majestic form.

(46) The Blessed Lord said, my dear friend, Arjuna,

    I am pleased to show this universal form of mine,

Which envelopes the whole creation, by my power and will,

    No one but you have seen,

    This dazzling magnificent and infinite vision of me.

(47) O best of warriors amongst the Kuru clan,

You are unique in seeing this form.

For by no means or by penance

Religious study or by sacrificial rites or great charities,

Can anyone see this Universal Form.

(48) Let not your mind be troubled,

By seeing this terrible aspect,

Of my supreme sovereignty.

There it is gone, be calm now.

The four armed form you desire

Is now apparent.

(49) Having seen such terrible form of mine

Do not be disturbed or confused,

Without fear and a peaceful mind,

Behold, once again, see my wonderful four armed form.
(With conch discuss mace and lotus flower

(50) Then Lord Krishna having spoken thus,
Revealed the four armed form to Arjuna,
And following this,
Resumed his charming two armed form,
To restore the spirits of his friend Arjuna.

(51) Arjuna then said,
On seeing the exquisitely beautiful,
Human form of Lord Krishna,
He was no longer afraid and became calm.
"My mind is now restored to peace,
Assuming its own nature,
O Janardana (chastiser of the enemy)"

The supreme God said,

(52) The angels and archangels always,
    Long to see this gentle human form,
    It is very difficult to see Me, my dear Arjuna,
    In this charming form of God.

(53) This My present form before you,
    Is impossible to see O Arjuna.
    Not by study of scripture (Vedas),
    Nor by penance,

Nor by charity or by worship,

Can one see Me as I am.

(54) Only with unconditional loving service and devotion,

Can I be known and seen directly,

As I am before you.

O mighty armed warrior,

Only by unconditional love can I be known as I am,

Or seen and entered into, O' Arjuna.

(55) O son of Pandu

He who doeth actions for me,

Who consider me the Supreme goal,

Who becomes my devotee, frees himself from all sins,

Such a man, with no personal enemy,

In unconditional love for all, comes to Me.

CHAPTER 12

The Yoga of Supreme Perfect Love

Lord Krishna and Arjuna

Arjuna spoke thus

(1) O' Krishna, please tell me,
   Of those who worship the Universal Spirit,
   The Unmanifested, Impersonal Supreme,
   And those who with unconditional love
   Constantly worship your eternal Divine Person,
   Of these two set of devotees,
   Who is more perfect?

(2) The Supreme Lord replies,
   Those devotees who with the purest and highest faith,
   Worship My personal form as God Supreme,
   Fixing their mind on me with unconditional love,
   Is the most perfect.

(3) But those who worship God as Spirit,
    Immaterial, imageless, all pervading, inconceivable,
    The permanent foundation of the universe,
    Beyond material sense perception,
    Can certainly attain to My being.

(4) These worship the impersonal, the Om,
    Representation of the Absolute truth,
    By self discipline over the senses,
    And faithfully engaged in
    Unconditional love and service to all beings.

(5) For those who are born into mortal bodies,
    And are attracted to the
    Impersonal formless Spirit of God,
    By the discipline of Yoga, fixing the mind,
    Is certainly more difficult.

(6) But those devotees who dedicate their life to Me
    In My personal identity,
    And make Me, the Supreme goal,
    Engaging in unalloyed unconditional love,
    For Me, with mind fixed on Me,
    I quickly bring salvation.

(7) I personally, O son of Pritha (Kunti),
    Swiftly deliver these worshippers,
    With unconditional love for Me,

From the ocean of birth and death.
For they have fixed their heart and soul in worshipping,
Me, the greatest of all beings.

(8) Just fix your mind on My personal form,
And utilize your intellect to find Me,
Thus you will dwell in Me always,
Of this there is no doubt.

(9) O Arjuna, if you cannot concentrate on Me,
Then follow the prescription of loving service to Me,
And thus you will develop,
A real desire to find Me.

(10) If O' Arjuna you fail to practice,
The description of unconditional devotional service,
And love (Yoga of love) for Me,
Then dedicate your life to My service,
And you will soon achieve perfection.

(11) Even if you are unable to dedicate your life to Me,
Then just act without seeking
Personal rewards and selfish results,
In a spirit of self discipline.

(12) Firstly, you may engage
In the pursuit of knowledge,
But better than knowledge is meditation,

Better than meditation is renunciation of self loving actions.

When one acts without selfishness,

One can attain unlimited peace.

(13) One who forgives and does not hate,

But is friendly and compassionate,

Who thinks nothing really belongs to him,

Who is free from selfishness and arrogance,

Who is poised in distress and happiness,

That person is very dear to Me.

(14) One who is always content and serene,

And engaged in unconditional love and service for Me,

Trying with great determination,

To discipline his heart and soul for Me,

Is very dear to Me.

(15) He who is not a trouble maker,

Who is calm in the face of trouble,

Without fear and anxiety,

Such a person is very dear to Me

(16) The person who is clean and pure,

Impartial and tranquil,

Free from all worries and distress,

And who refrains from selfish endeavors,
This devotee is very dear to Me.

(17) He who is calm and never rejoices or hate,
Never craving or lamenting,
Who is steady in the face of good or evil,
This, my devotee is very dear to Me.

(18) That devotee who treats friends and enemies alike,
Who is steady in heat or cold, joy or sorrow,
And does not crave company,
Is very dear to Me.

(19) He who is indifferent to fame or blame,
Who is silent with peace in his heart,
Who is happy with no matter what,
Who does not care about domestic residence,
Such a devotee of mine,
Fixed in serving Me with love,
Is very dear to Me

(20) He who worships Me,
Following this path of love and service,
And who with transcendental faith,
Makes Me the highest goal of his life
That exalted devotee, is very dear to Me.

CHAPTER 13

Creation and the Lord of Creation

Lord Supreme Vishnu

(1) O Keshava,

I wish to know

About the phenomenal world,

Of Mother Nature,

And the Supreme Master of this phenomenal Nature

To know about this body,

And the one who understands this body,

To know what is real knowledge,

And the main purpose of knowledge.

(2) The blessed God Krishna then said,

This material body is called the field,

And one who understands this body,

Is the real knower of the field.

(3) O son of the dynasty of King Bharata,

Please understand that God Supreme,

Has knowledge of all existing bodies.
Information regarding this body and
Its governors are real knowledge.

(4) Now let Me describe this field as it is,
What changes occur,
How they come about in detail,
What are the influences of this field,
And who is the knower of this field.

(5) The great savant sages,
Have previously, in the Vedic hymns,
Described variously in a scientific way,
Especially in the Vedanta Sutra,
Concluding portions of the Veda,
The, who, where, when and why
Of this phenomenal nature, and its Master.

(6) The great expression of gross matter,
Solid, liquid, gas, electricity and space,
The ego, intellect, the unmanifested substances (pradhana),
The ten senses and mind,
The five sense objects of hearing seeing, feeling,
Tasting and smelling are described.

(7) Desire and hate, happiness and distress,
The aggregate of living symptoms,
Will and determination,

All these activities and their interactions,
Are operations in this field or body.

(8) What is knowledge is here described,
Humility, lack of false pride, non violence,
Peacefulness and tolerance with simplicity,
Seeking an enlightened teacher,
Purity, continuous efforts and sense control.

(9) Renunciation of sensual indulgence,
Arrogance and conceit,
Perceiving the futility of death,
Birth, old age and suffering.

(10) Doing one's duty,
To children, spouse, family and home,
Without selfishness,
Always poised in both favorable and difficult situations.

(11) Devoted to Me,
Continuously in love,
Living in a solitary place,
Avoiding crowds and social attachment.

(12) Fixed in pursuit of self realization,
And the finding of the absolute truth.
All this is considered knowledge,

Anything opposed to these is ignorance.

(13) I shall now O Arjuna, explain to you,
   Real knowledge, knowing which,
   You will taste the nectar of the eternal.
   This eternal is without origin.
   It is under my control,
   And it is Brahman or spirit soul
   It is untouched by the material qualities of Nature.

(14) This all pervading Spirit,
   Is multi present and multi potential.
   He has everywhere hands and legs,
   Everywhere eyes and faces.
   He hears everything and He envelopes all.

(15) This super-soul is the origin,
   Of all the gunas (qualities of Nature).
   He has no sense organs
   Yet he is the supreme support of the universe.
   He transcends material Nature,
   He is without form or image,
   Yet is master of all forms.

(16) This supreme principle,
   Is within and outside all beings,
   Simultaneously, even in inanimate things,

He is not perceptible to the ordinary senses,
Although he is remote, yet he is quite near.

(17) Although he is a unity,
   He may seem divided,
   But is always indivisible,
   Paradoxically while being the mountain of all things,
   Yet he produces and devours all things.

(18) This Super-soul is the source of all light,
   He is not apparent.
   He is beyond the power of darkness,
   He is knowledge, to be known by knowledge,
   And the goal of knowledge,
   He is present in every heart.

(19) Thus the field and the knower of the field,
   Has been described by Me in total,
   My loving devotee, understanding this mystery,
   Attains to My true Nature.

(20) Material Nature (Prakrith) and intelligent life (Purusha)
   Must be considered eternal,
   Also the permutations and combinations,
   In natural processes are eternal,

(21) In this creation, Nature becomes
   The instrument of cause and effect,

    Whereas intelligent life causes,

    Sorrows, happiness and enjoyment

    In this world according to law (Karma).

(22) This soul dwelling in this body

    Is identical with the Supreme.

    He is said to be the eternal Witness,

    The true Director, the maintainer of all,

    The one who truly experiences everything,

    The Supreme Overlord,

And the absolute God as well.

(23) Intelligent life attached to Nature,

    Experiences through the agencies

    Of goodness, passion and ignorance,

    The resulting happiness and evil

    Associated with Natural Law,

    In various species.

(24) Yet within this intelligent being (life)

    There is another being called Parmatma

    Who is Supreme and is God within

    He is the Master beneficiary,

    Supervisor and Lord.

(25) One who truly comprehends,

    Intelligent life and blind Nature and God within,

    And the operation of the forces,

And laws of harmony, activity and inertia,

And their moral counterparts,

Goodness, passion and ignorance,

Is sure to become free,

He will never again be born in ignorance (avidya).

(26) This God within, this Super-soul,

Can be perceived by science,

By the system of yoga and meditation,

By the engagement in unselfish,

Unconditional love and service for others,

Without seeking personal rewards.

(27) O Arjuna, chief of the Bharata Dynasty,

Whatever there is in this universe,

Both stationery and mobile,

Know that, to be a combination of Spirit and matter,

Intelligent life and nature

The field and the knower of the field.

(28) This Paramatma, God within

Is equally present everywhere,

In all intelligent life,

He who sees that both the individual soul

And the supersoul is never destroyed,

Truly understands reality,

(29) The super consciousness of one,

Who perceives God within,

Present everywhere, pervading the universe,

Never descends to mundane consciousness.

In this state, he enters

The kingdom of God

(30) Those who see that all actions,

Are carried out by this mortal body,

A creation of Material Nature,

And that both Spirit and Supreme Spirit are inactive,

Such a person has achieved true vision.

(31) When the enlightened sage,

Perceives the Divinity of the Whole Universe,

And ceases to see individual and separated beings,

He rises to the level of Brahman consciousness (super consciousness in divinity).

(32) With this superior vision of transcendence,

Above the operation of Material Nature

And consciousness not identified with the body,

One sees that Spirit or soul is free,

It does nothing and nothing can affect it.

(33) The sky and space so rarefied,

Though present everywhere,

Mixes with nothing.

So too the liberated soul,

Free from material consciousness,

And situated in God consciousness,

Is untouched by the material body,

Though dwelling within it.

(34) O son of Bharata,

As the sun though one,

Fills this universe with light,

So too, does the soul,

Make conscious the entire body,

Of the living being.

(35) The enlightened being,

Who can clearly see,

The difference between body and soul,

Spirit and matter,

And knows how to extricate himself,

From the bondage of material consciousness,

Can achieve his liberation,

And my Supreme Abode.

CHAPTER 14

Mother Sprit
and the Three qualities of Nature

God as Shakti- Power

My dear Arjuna

(1) Again I converse with you,

About the highest wisdom,

And best of knowledge.

The great sages with their enlightenment,

Achieved the highest perfections possible.

(2) By accepting the shelter

Of this superior knowledge and consciousness,

One can become like unto Me and My very nature.

In this transcendental position,

One is never again born into this material world,

Or die at its inevitable end.

(3) This cosmic universe is the source of all life,

It is called Brahman

And I am the Father, who plants the seed,
Making possible the birth of all living beings
In this universe.

(4) O son of Kunti,
Behold, I am the Father
Who gives impetus,
And makes possible,
The birth of every species.
I provide the seed to this proliferation of life.

(5) The universe comes about
By the operation of three agents,
In material, nature, harmony, activity and inertia
And their moral counterparts
Goodness, passion and ignorance.
When the immortal soul comes in contact.
With blind nature, it assumes qualities of these modalities.

(6) O sinless Arjuna,
The quality of goodness is superior and purer.
When one assumes such a character,
One refrains from sin,
Is more enlightened,
One becomes happy,
But becomes enamored of this kind of life.

(7) When a soul assumes
    The character of passion
    He is wildly active, passionate,
    Greedy, lusty and acquisitive.
    His life is an expression of self love,
    To which he becomes entangled.

(8) The quality of ignorance,
    Pre-dispose the individual,
    To spiritual ignorance and delusion,
    To laziness and mental instability,
    His life is at the level of a beast.

(9) The good person
    Is relatively happy,
    The man of passion is selfish,
    And acquisitive,
    The person in ignorance is unstable and mad.

(10) The character of each individual,
    Is dependent on the predominance of each quality,
    That constantly competes with each other,
    Sometimes goodness prevails
    At other times, passion and ignorance.

(11) When goodness prevails,
    The individual is spiritually aware,

The light of a higher knowledge pervades his life,
And he sees things in greater reality.

(12) When the mode of passion
    Is predominant
    Selfish love, desires, cravings,
     And ambitions possess the individual.

(13) O son of Kunti
    The quality of ignorance,
     Exhibits as madness,
    Delusion, darkness,
    Stubbornness and slothfulness.

(14) A man dying in the mode of goodness,
    Reaches the planets,
    Of angels and archangels,
    Sages and the godly.

(15) Dying in the mode of passion
    One again appears,
    Among people dedicated to selfish activities.
    Dying in the mode of ignorance,
    Leads to criminal existence in the next life.

(16) If your life,
Follows the path of goodness,
Then you become purer.

A life in the mode of passion, leads to sorrow.

(17) From the mode of goodness,
   Spiritual knowledge and enlightenment results.
   From the mode of passion, troubles, grief and failures
   From the mode of ignorance
   Confusion, waste and darkness.

(18) Living in the mode of goodness,
   One is elevated to higher planets (angels),
   That in the mode of passion leads to human life,
   And in the mode of ignorance
   One descends into hell.

(19) A man who perceives,
   That the whole universe
   Is the field of activity,
   Of the three modes or qualities of Nature,
   And that the Super-soul,
   Is eternally aloof from these modes,
   Such a man can understand my true Nature.

(20) When, one living in a mortal body,
   Can overcome the influence
   Of these three modes of Nature,
   He attains victory over birth,
   Death, old age and sorrow,
   And can, in this very life

Enjoy the nectar of self realization.

(21) Arjuna asked,

How can I distinguish a man of wisdom,

Who has transcended these material modes?

And how does he overcome these modes?

The Lord said:

(22) He who is indifferent to selfish love,

Illusion and non spiritual education,

Whether present or not

With no hate or craving for such.

(23) He is in a position of neutrality

He is not affected,

By the forces of the modes of nature,

He is firm and steady in his course

(24) The man free from the Gunas,

Knows they are causes,

For the transformation of Nature.

Hence he is indifferent,

To pain and material pleasures,

He looks on gold, stone and soil, in the same light.

He is steady,

And equally is unaffected,

By praise or blame, honor and dishonor,

(25) He is steady if honored and steady if ignored,

He treats friend and enemy alike,

He no longer strives for selfish love or rewards.

Such an elevated sage

Has transcended the modes of Nature.

(26) Unconditional love and service to Me

Is the hallmark of this Man of Freedom.

He undoubtedly goes,

Beyond the realm of the modes of Nature,

And is transported to the level of divine consciousness

(27) For I am the eternal foundation,

Of the supreme Brahman,

All pervading, Supreme, Spirit of God.

I am the fountain of Ultimate Happiness,

(Immortality and Eternity)

CHAPTER 15

Knowing God the Supreme
Person the Perfect Being

God Supreme Lord Vishnu

(1) There is an eternal Banyan tree,

    Whose branches drop downwards,

    But whose roots rise upwards.

    The Vedas are the leaves of this tree

    One who knows this tree is an expert in the Vedas

(2) The branches of this tree, (tree reflected in water)

    Go downwards and turn upwards,

  And are sustained by the Three Modes of Material Nature,

    The twigs of these branches are the goals of sensual life,

    Roots from the tree also go down,

  But these are fixed to the self loving acts of human beings.

(3) So extensive is the banyan tree, (universal)

    No one can visualize it,

    It is without beginning and without end.

(And without foundation)
This banyan tree is powerfully anchored by its roots.
But my dear Arjuna,
You must with great willpower,
Slash down this tree,
By the weapon of renunciation.

(4) Henceforth you must seek
That from which,
There is no return to darkness.
You will surrender to the great Lord,
That Primal Person,
Who is the very source and
Sustenance of this great universe.

(5) That individual who is enlightened,
Free from the illusion,
Of self-loving attachment.
And to honor and bad company indifferent.
Who has conquered his cravings and lusts,
And transcended the duality of happiness and darkness,
Enters into the Kingdom of God.

(6) In this self luminous,
Supreme abode of Mine,
There is so sun, moon or stars,

No electricity or fire,
No light, but the light of God.

(7) The living souls are manifestations,
   Of my eternal minute existences.
   Because of their delusional,
   Separate and selfish identity,
   Life becomes a great struggle,
   Against senses and mind.

(8) As a gentle breeze carries,
   The aroma of flowers in its path,
   So too does the living soul,
    On leaving the body,
   Carry the essence of his earthly life
   To the next bodily existence.

(9) The soul on acquiring another body,
   Exhibits the sensitivities and preferences,
   Of taste, touch, smell and sight for enjoyment.
   His concept and philosophy of life
   Is embedded in his new mind.

(10) The impure and unenlightened,
   Blind to transcendental knowledge,
   Have no clue,
   As to the transmigration of souls,

And the operation of the Modes of Nature.
But the wise man can see this clearly.

(11) The yogi in communion with the Supreme,
Can witness this phenomenon clearly.
But those souls steeped in materialism,
Cannot see this, even with great effort.

(12) Because from Me comes the Sun,
Whose light destroys the darkness,
Behold, I am the splendor of the Moon,
Of electricity and fire,
I am the light of the world.

(13) In every planet of the universe,
I enter,
I sustain all living things.
By the power of Divine Energy,
I become the dew drops in moonlight,
To make luscious all vegetables.

(14) I am the fire of oxidation,
In all living beings,
I am present in every breath,
And through Me,
Assimilation of all foods
Take place.

(15) O' Arjuna

    I am the Lord,

    Seated in the heart of all beings,

    From me alone come memory,

    Knowledge and loss of memory.

    I am the author of all the Vedas

    I composed the Vedanta, by this knowledge,

     You can know Me certainly.

(16) Apart from God Supreme,

    There are two types of living beings,

    The perishable and the imperishable.

    Those subject to mortal death,

    People the material world.

   The imperishable beings constitute the spiritual universe.

(17) But the Lord of all beings

    Of the spiritual and material worlds,

    Is God Supreme,

    The best and highest of all personalities,

    Creating, maintaining and regulating this universe.

(18) Because I am superior O Arjuna,

    To both the perishable and imperishable,

   And because I am the best and most elevated of all beings,

    The Vedas and people,

Proclaim my fame as Purushottama,
The highest and best of all personalities.

(19) He, who,
Without a doubt in his mind,
Truly knows me as Purushottama,
The best of all beings,
Can then worship Me,
With all his heart and soul and might,
This state is the summit of all wisdom.

(20) O sinless Arjuna,
I have now revealed to you,
The most confidential,
 And most secret of all scriptures.
By understanding this knowledge,
One can gain wisdom,
And succeed in all his ventures.

(21) Arjuna said, how can we recognize
A man who has risen above the three gunas?
How does he act, and how does he rise above the three
gunas?

(22) Lord Krishna said
O Arjuna, he who does not hate light
Which is born of satva and action
Which is born of rajas

Or even inertia, born of tamas when present
Nor longs for them when they are absent

(23) The man who, neutral like a witness
Is not disturbed by the gunas
And knows that the gunas alone are active
Remains firmly in his identity with God Supreme,
And never alters from that state.

(24) He who is always established
In union with the Supreme,
Treats pain and pleasure alike
Looks upon a piece of dirt
As stone or gold of equal value.
This person is wise,
He accepts the pleasant just as he accepts the unpleasant,
And considers praise and blame alike

(25) This person has risen above the three gunas,
Who is the same in fame and blame
Is alike towards a friend or enemy
And does not consider himself the actor, the doer of things

(26) That person who continuously worships me exclusively
By the yoga of devotion,
Rising above the three gunas
Is fit to enter the kingdom of Brahman

(27) For I Myself am the foundation of the Supreme Brahman,

　　Unmanifest, Supreme Spirit,

　　I am the foundation of immortality,

　　The eternal dharma

　　And absolute happiness.

CHAPTER 16

The Divine and the Demonic Qualities

RAVAN TEN HEADED DEMON

O scion of the Bharata race,

These are the qualities of great men, **GOD SUPREME VISHNU**

Born with the talents of divine action.

(1) Fearlessness, purity,

Spiritual understanding

Focus on the Supreme!

Making sacrifices, study of scriptures (Veda),

Austerity and simplicity.

(2) Non violence, truthfulness, control of anger,

Renunciation of selfishness and self love,

Peacefulness, cessation of fault finding,

Compassion and sweetness,

Clearing of the heart from greed,
Modesty, steadfastness (courage, forgiveness).

(3) Drive, cleanliness,
No envy or jealousy,
Abolishing the craving and passion for honor,
These are the talents of men,
With divine proclivities.

(4) The ungodly, and evil O Partha,
Are born with these qualities.
False pride, conceit and arrogance
Harshness, anger and denial of truth.

(5) The divine qualities,
Are conducive to salvation,
And realization of the absolute truth.
Ungodly qualities are found,
In evil men bound for hell.
Fear not my friend,
You were born with divine qualities,

(6) In this creation, O son of Pritha
There exist two classes of beings,
One the godly, the other evil.
I have described to you the divine qualities,
Now hear about the evil ones.

(7) The ungodly and evil knows not,

    What duty is or what is forbidden,

    They are not pure or clean,

    They are lawless and lying,

    They cannot adhere to truth or keep promises.

(8) They say,

    That there is no God,

    That there is no transcendent reality,

    No foundation than what they see,

    No supreme controller.

    Lust and ambition,

    The survival of the fittest,

    Is their philosophy of life.

(9) The spiritually blind,

    Accepting this philosophy,

    Have abandoned their heritage (soul).

    They are lost in evil,

    War and destruction,

    Suppression and self indulgence,

    Threatening the whole world with annihilation.

(10) Mad with lust, conceit and arrogance,

    And filled with unhealthy pride,

    These lost souls, deluded of men,

    Vow to create havoc

In the temporary affairs of men,

(11) Sensual gratification is their goal of life,
With this lifestyle,
They are filled with great fear and worries,
Prepared to die for these pleasures.

(12) Enveloped in hundreds of thousands,
Of lusts, desires, cravings and anger,
They steal from others,
And bank for their own needs.

(13) This much money,
I have gained today,
And with my schemes,
I shall even be richer.

(14) Many foes have I killed today,
And soon I shall kill others,
I am in control, powerful and expert,
I will enjoy and be really happy.

(15) Who is like unto me?
I will enjoy,
I am famous, surrounded by wealth
And beautiful family
I shall create ritual ceremonies (yagna) for show,
And publicize my charities,

This is the height of spiritual,
Ignorance and delusion.

(16) To hell O' Arjuna, descend these souls,
Bound by hundreds of self loving desires.
In this net of illusions and delusions,
They fall flat in the abyss of doom.

(17) Pompously confident and,
Shamelessly insulting,
Steeped in self importance,
And the prestige of wealth,
They create sacrifices in name only,
Dismissing rules and regulations of worship.

(18) These demons among men,
In great envy of Me,
Egoistic and confused,
Deluded by pride, lust and anger,
Makes blasphemy against My person,
Present in their own heart (and in the soul of other men).

(19) These lowest of the lowest,
Envious and evil,
By my law, I project into hell,
Into the wombs of dastardly,
Devilish and demonic species.

(20) Birth after birth,

    Atheistic and demonic species,

    These spiritual fools,

    Cannot approach Me.

    They descend again and again,

    Into the darkness of hell.

(21) Lust, anger and greed,

    Are the three gates of hell

    Every sane man,

    Must avoid these three,

    Renouncing evil and selfish love,

    To prevent the ruin of his own sweet soul.

(22) That fortunate man,

    Who escapes these three gates of hell,

    Becomes absorbed in acts of love,

    Without selfishness,

    And focus on Me.

    He soon achieves the kingdom of God.

(23) Those who arrogantly dismisses,

    Discipline and laws,

    Laid down in scriptures,

    But act only to satisfy their own,

    Natural lusts and desires,

Cannot achieve happiness,

Success or blessings of God Supreme.

(24) With the scriptures as your guide,

You should determine,

What is your right duty,

And what is not.

With such enlightened knowledge,

You must do your duty with love.

CHAPTER 17

The Three fold nature of Faith

Arjuna asked,

(1) For those who disregards,
    Scriptural rules and regulations
    Creating his own faith,
    In what characteristic Mode of Nature,
    Does he fall O Lord?
    In goodness passion or ignorance.

(2) The blessed Lord said,
    Depending upon their past lives,
    Men are born,
    Into one of the three expressions (faith)
    Of the Modes of Nature,
    Of goodness, passion, ignorance.
    Now listen to me of these.

(3) One's faith is dependent
   On the inheritance of one
   Of these qualities (Gunas of nature)
   A man's faith evolves,
   From this particular quality of matter.

(4) People in the mode of goodness
   Often sacrifice,
   To the controllers of this universe,
   Angels and Archangels.
   Those in the mode of passion,
   Please demons and satans.
   And those in the quality of spiritual ignorance (actually)
   Sacrifice to ghosts and spirits.

(5) Motivated by forceful arrogance,
   Lust and selfish aims,
   Some ungodly satanic beings,
   Perform frightful penances,
   And acts of austerities,
    Against the rules of scripture.

(6) In their conceit and mode of nature,
   They torture their own bodies,
   And insult God within their own soul.
   Such creatures are qualified as ungodly.

(7) The faith of each man and his quality
     Can be distinguished,
     By the food he loves, listen to Me
     The type of sacrifice, austerity and charity
     Delineates, his place in the realm of Nature

(8) Foods liked by those in Goodness (virtue)
     Are soft, tasty, juicy and healthy
     They increase life, strength and happiness,
     Giving pleasure and delight in eating.

(9) Sour, bitter, hot and salty
     Burning, dry and very sharp,
     These are foods in the Mode of Passion
     Source or sorrow, sickness and suffering

(10) Foods quite stale, old and tasteless,
      Decomposing, foul smelling and leavings
      These are dear to those poor souls,
      Born in the mode of ignorance and darkness.

(11) Any one who performs a sacrifice
      Without seeking personal reward,
      Does so in the mode of goodness,
      He does his duty as prescribed.

(12) O warrior of the Bharata clan,
      Sacrifice performed just for show,

With selfish interest and conceit,
That sacrifice is in the mode of passion

(13) That sacrifice against scriptural rules,
   And without Vedic prayers,
   That ceremony without distribution of offerings,
   And no gifts to priests and saints,
   That sacrifices without faith
   Is in the mode of darkness

(14) Purity, simplicity, continence and celibacy
   Non violence to all creatures
   These consist of austerity of the body
   Devotion to God,
   Saintly teachers and Brahmanas
   Also constitute the austerity of this body

(15) Speaking the truth,
   Speaking sweetly and cheerfully,
   And for the benefit of others,
   And reciting regularly the Vedic prayers,
   Is considered austerity of speech.

(16) Penance of the mind,
   Is contentment and peace,
   Without scheme or guile
   Silence, self control,
   Serenity and purity,

Denote, penance of the mind.

(17) The threefold austerity described by me
  In the mode of goodness
  Is to please Me, God Supreme,
  It is done without self loving goals,
  And without seeking personal rewards.

(18) Those who perform penances,
  Just for show,
  To gain fame, name and respect,
  These activities are in the mode of passion
  Fleeting and insignificant.

(19) The foolish who perform,
  Self torture as penance,
  To cause injury or destruction
  Is said to be in the mode
Of ignorance and darkness.

(20) That gift given,
  Without seeking reward,
  To a needy and appropriate person,
  Is considered as one,
  In the mode of goodness.

(21) That gift given reluctantly,
  Or for self blessing or reward,

Is considered by Me to be
Charity in the nature of passion.

(22) That charity devoid of respect,
And given carelessly,
At an improper time and place,
To an unworthy recipient
Is clearly in the mode of ignorance.

(23) Om Tat Sat represent the supreme designator,
Of the absolute truth in these three words.
Since the time of creation,
Holiness, scriptures and sacred sacrifice,
Arose out of this primal hymn.

(24) The holy enlightened beings,
Always commence all sacrifices,
Charity and penance,
With this holy syllable OM,
Following this tradition

(25) One who seeks salvation,
Must utter Tat,
In all acts of sacrifice,
Austerity and charity.

(26) The word Sat represents
The sound of unconditional

Unselfish love of God,
O son of Pritha

(27) Pure sacrifice,
Austerity and charity,
Is represented too,
In the word Sat
These acts are truly meant,
To please God
OM TAT SAT.

(28) If an oblation is offered in the fire
A gift is given, a hardship is practiced,
And whatever good a man may do,
If it is without faith and love,
It is called "Asat"
Therefore without faith even a good activity,
Is of no avail or useless.

CHAPTER 18

Finding God Supreme by Perfection in knowledge and Devotion

FINDING GOD

(1) Arjuna spoke to the Lord of the senses (Krishna).

Dear Krishna, I wish to know

What is the true meaning,

Of renunciation,

And the different interpretations,

Of this order of life (sanyasa).

(2) The Blessed Lord said,

The wise define renunciation,

As giving up all activities,

Born of selfish desires,

While those in the order of renunciation,

Define renunciation,

As giving up and not seeking personal rewards.

(3) Some savants declare,

    That all actions should be given up as evil.

    While others say,

    That acts of worship,

    Penance and charity,

    Should never be abandoned

(4) O best of the dynasty of Bharata,

    Please learn from Me about renunciation.

    Certainly, O tiger among men,

    I have described three kinds of renunciation.

(5) Sacrifice, austerity and charity,

    Must be performed as duty,

    And not abandoned,

    For these are purifying acts,

    Even for great souls.

(6) Certainly these purifying acts,

    Should be performed,

    Without selfish motives,

    Or expectation of reward.

    They must be part of your duty,

    This is My final and certain conclusion.

(7) Duties designated (from talent and training)

    Should never be abandoned.

    If by delusion one abandons his duty,

This is considered as action,
In the mode of ignorance.

(8) He who relinquishes his duty,
    Because he thinks it is difficult or dangerous,
    Acts in the mode of passion
    These are not acts of selfless renunciation.

(9) But he who acts as he is trained to do,
    Because he must, as his duty,
    Without seeking personal reward,
    Acts in the mode of goodness O' Arjuna.

(10) Those higher souls,
    In the mode of goodness,
    Who does not hate their duty,
    Nor act selfishly doing their duty,
    Know what duty is without doubts.

(11) Impossible indeed it is,
    For those in mortal bodies,
    To abandon all activities.
    But those who renounce selfish action,
    Seeking no personal reward,
Are certainly engaged in renunciation.

(12) Those who practice not true renunciation,
    Are subject to the three fold reactions,

Good bad and mixed,
Accruing after death,
But those who have renounced selfish interest,
Are free from such Karmic reactions.

(13) Dear Arjuna,
Please learn from me
Of the five Vedic factors
To bring about,
Perfection in all action.

(14) They are,
The character of the performance,
The various instruments of action,
The place of action,
The efforts,
And finally the allowance,
Or sanction of God Supreme.

(15) Action performed by body,
Speech or mind,
Whether right or wrong deeds,
Are all caused by these five factors.

(16) But he who considers himself,
The sole actor,
Without acknowledging the other factors,

Is lacking in intelligence,
And full of ignorance.

(17) He who never acts from selfish motives
    Whose heart is not steeped in self love,
    Though he kills men,
    In his duty as warrior,
    Is not really a murderer,
    And is not guilty of sin.

(18) Information,
    The aim of information,
    And the informer himself,
    Are the factors which motivate action.
    The information used,
    The work to be done,
    And the worker,
Culminate in the execution of action.

(19) O' Arjuna
    With respect to the three modes of nature
    There exist three kinds of knowledge,
    Three sets of actions,
    And three types of performers.
    Now listen to my description.

(20) That knowledge by which
    One sees spiritual unity in all beings,

And the imperishable soul,

As the foundation of this manifold universe,

That knowledge is in the mode of goodness.

(21) But one who sees multiplicity alone,

In countless beings,

Without perceiving the underlying unity,

Has knowledge in the mode of passion.

(22) But one who sees no further,

Than his self centered existence,

And becomes attached to his selfish work,

Without enlightenment or depth of knowledge,

Is considered to be in the mode of darkness.

(23) Of actions, O Arjuna,

That action that follows discipline,

That is selfless,

Without attachment or hatred,

And without seeking personal reward,

Is action in the mode of goodness

(24) Motivated by selfish ambitions,

And craving for personal distinctions,

And when performed with tremendous effort,

This action is in the mode of passion.

(25) That action carelessly enacted,

    Without thought of consequences to others,

    Of harming, distressing or violence to them,

    And without regard to its inherent sin,

    This action is in the mode of darkness.

(26) That worker is in the mode of goodness,

Who becomes free from selfish ambition,

    He has renounced,

    Seeking personal rewards,

    He enjoys his work,

    Immune to success or failure,

    He is resolute on the exccution of his duty,

(27) But that worker greedy for results

    Envy and jealousy, his personal lifestyle,

    Joy and sorrow, routine experiences,

    That impure person,

    Is in the mode of passion.

(28) But he who is not devoted to principles,

    Who is stubborn and materialistic,

    Vulgar, unreliable and lazy,

    In bad moods, often procrastinating,

    Such a person is in the mode of darkness.

(29) O winner of wealth, Arjuna,

    Let me tell you in detail,

Of the three kinds of reasonings,

And resolve arising from them,

According to the modes of material nature.

(30) What is right, and what is wrong,

What is duty and what not,

What to fear and what to love,

What frees the mind and what enslaves it,

A man with such intellectual capacity,

Is in the mode of goodness

(31) And that reasoning mind,

Which finds difficulty,

In ascertaining what is godly,

And what is ungodly,

What is duty,

And what is against duty,

That imperfect faculty,

Is of the mode of passion

(32) That intellect O Arjuna,

Which confuses religion with evil,

Who is steeped in ignorance and illusion

Resolving always to the wrong side

Is reasoning in the mode of darkness

(33) O son of Kunti

That determination which is resolute,

In a life disciplined by yoga
Controlling ones energy, mind and senses
That resolve is in the mode of goodness

(34) And that resolve,
Which is imbedded with selfishness
Greedy for fame, love and wealth,
That determination is,
In the mode of passion (Rajas)

(35) And that person of weak character
Who cannot transcend
His dreams, fears, depression, confusion
And constantly complaining,
Possesses, determination
In the mode of ignorance (Tamasa)

(36) There exist three kinds of happiness
Corresponding to the three modes of Nature,
Which the individual enjoys
And which may finally lead him
To final freedom from sorrows.

(37) That pleasure which is at first,
Like the bitter taste of poison,
But later changes into honey,
That pleasure of transcendental truth,

Is happiness in the mode of goodness.

(38) That joy of sensual pleasures
Which is like nectar in the beginning,
But later becomes bitter as poison
That happiness is called
The happiness of passion

(39) And that happiness
Which is oblivious to,
The potential of the soul
And the joy of knowing God,
And which results,
In a character of spiritual sleep,
Ignorance and apathy,
Is certainly in the mode of darkness

(40) No individual among humans,
Angels or archangels
Higher or lower beings,
In this whole cosmic universe
Is completely free from the influence
Of these three modes of material nature
Satva, Tamas and Rajas

(41) The four castes of human society,
Are distinguished also
By the talents they inherit,

At the time of birth
Corresponding to the modes of material nature
O Arjuna, Brahamanas,
Kshattriyas, Vaishas and Shudras
Like natural divisions of human society
(And not hereditary structures and confusions).

(42) Brahamanas, spiritual leaders are characterized,
    By purity and forgiveness,
    Peacefulness and discipline
    Honesty and Austerity,
    Knowledge and wisdom

(43) Executive leaders called Kshattriyas (warriors)
    Are men of courage, drive and power,
    Resolute, resourceful, fearless in battle
    Generous and heroic leaders among men,
    Their talents are inherited from nature and forbears

(44) Agriculture and farming
    Production of milk and cattle,
    Commerce and business
    Characterize the talents of Vaishas
    While excellence in service,
    In labor and support
    Are the talents distinguishing,
    The cast of Sudras

(45) By following his own inherited talent,
    Nature of quality and aptitude
    Everyone who follows duly and
    With excellence,
    Becomes perfect.
    Please hear from me, how this is done.

(46) A man who worships God Supreme,
    The Lord who pervades this whole universe,
    And is source of all things,
    Thus striving for excellence,
    In his own duty to God
    Can achieve perfection

(47) It is better to do one's duty,
    For which one is endowed by nature,
    Thought it may be imperfect (for a time),
    Than to strive to do the duty of another.
    Without that talent in aptitude
    Tho it can be done perfectly (temporarily).
    Doing one's duty according to talent,
    Training and aptitude incurs no sin.

(48) Every attempt to work
    Can have errors or faults O Arjuna
    Just as clear fire,
    Is covered by smoke.
    Hence every man should seek excellence

In the occupation suited,

To his talent and training,

Even when this course is,

Not the easiest way.

(49) With the philosophy of unselfish love,

And mind controlled by discipline

Renouncing, material desires,

And seeking perfection,

In unconditional loving service and selflessness

A man attains the highest elevation

Of renunciation (Sanyasa)

(50) O son of Kunti,

Let me in brief show you,

How one can achieve

The perfection of cosmic consciousness,

The final destination of the soul,

Into the oneness of God Supreme.

(51) To know God in truth,

One's intellect must become purified.

One must be focused with determination

On finding the truth,

In a process of discipline and purity.

He must renounce attachments to sensual joys,

Freeing oneself from selfishness and hatred.

(52) Living in solitude, eating sparingly,
    Controlling body, mind and speech,
    Absorbed in God consciousness,
    Always detached from the temptations of life
    One can realize God.

(53) Such a person is free from egoism,
    Free from false pride, craving for things,
    Controlling his passion and anger
    Always peaceful and serene,
    This person has become elevated
    To the realization of the Truth.

(54) The man in Supreme consciousness
    Has achieved self realization,
    And his unity with God Supreme.
    He does not crave, he does not worry
    He is impartial to all living beings.
    In that state of great love
    Unconditional, unselfish,
    Universal love for Me
    He becomes transcendentally transported to My abode

(55) By such unconditional love and service,
    My devotee can find,
    The Highest Truth about Me

And find Me as I am truly
With this transcendental consciousness.

(56) By my grace O' Arjuna
My devotee lives under my protection
And though he seemingly
Engages in multiple activities,
Finally reaches My supreme eternal destination.

(57) Work under My protection,
Depend on Me always,
And fix your mind on Me
In wise and loving devotion.

(58) If you fix your mind in Me
I will, by My grace
Help you overcome,
All the problems of life.
But if you do not listen and act selfishly,
Ignoring My advice,
You shall destroy yourself.

(59) O Arjuna,
If through selfish love,
You refuse to fight,
Not listening to me

You will fail by your false reasoning,
And nature will force you to fight anyway.

(60) O Arjuna you now refuse in delusion,
To obey my divine direction,
But by the talents and training,
Arising from your own inherent qualities,
You will inevitably fight.

(61) The Supreme Controller, God Supreme
Dwells in the heart of all beings, O Arjuna
By law, he directs their lives
And they sit in the train of cosmic journey.

(62) O scion of Bharata,
Surrender in love to this Lord,
With all your heart.
By his grace, you shall attain eternal peace
And enter into the kingdom of God.

(63) I have now revealed to you
The most confidential and most secret of secrets.
Meditate on it completely,
Then make your decision O Arjuna.

(64) Once more listen to Me,
To this most confidential secret science,
You are indeed dear to Me,

And I give you this instruction
For your benefit

(65) Fix your mind on Me,
And love Me unconditionally,
Bow down to Me and worship Me.
There is no doubt you will come to Me,
I promise you truly,
For you are My dearest friend.

(66) Whatever you have heard of religion before,
You should abandon now,
Just surrender to Me as your only refuge,
I will save you from all sins,
And give you salvation,
Do not fear.

(67) This highest spiritual knowledge
Should not be revealed,
To those who are faithless,
Against loving service to God,
Who is an enemy of Truth and God Supreme,
And who doubts or fights against,
My Sovereignty and Supremacy.

(68) That devotee of mine,
Who reveals this supreme confidential science,
Of unconditional loving service to God,

Must be considered to have performed
The greatest service to Me
And without doubt he will attain Me.

(69) Of all devotees
He who reveals this science,
And My glory to others,
Is very dear to Me.
No one shall be dearer to Me than he.

(70) And I say to you
That those who study,
This our divine discourse,
Worships Me with,
The sacrifice of his intelligence,
This is my definite conclusion!

(71) And one who listens with firm faith
And with a spirit of acceptance and not rejection,
Even he freed from sins
Will attain the abode of the virtuous

(72) Dhananjaye, Conqueror of wealth,
Have you received this message,
With undivided attention,
Are your doubts and misgivings now vanished,
(Do you understand your duty and devotion)?

(73) Arjuna declared,

    I understand and remember,

     Who I am in truth.

    My illusions and misconceptions are gone,

    By thy grace, O infallible Lord,

    My doubts have vanished and I am determined to act,

    I shall obey you completely O My God.

(74) Sanjaya, the servant of the blind king then said

    Thus did I, Sanjay,

    Hear and witness, this holy dialogue,

    Between Lord Krishna and the noble Arjuna.

    So marvelous was that conversation,

    That the hairs on my body stand up.

(75) By the mercy of the Sage Vyaasa,

    I have personally witnessed and listened,

    To the most confidential and secret,

    Mystic doctrine of the Supreme,

    By the Lord of Yoga himself,

    The Supreme Lord Krishna.

(76) And my heart is filled with joy,

    Again and again, O King Dhritrashta

    When I remember this beauteous,

    Wondrous, dialogue

Between the Lord of all creations, Krishna,
And his pious devotee, Arjuna

(77) And when I evoke the memory,
Of this majestic wonder of wonders, Lord Hari,
His magnificent universal form,
My heart beats with joy,
Again and time again.

(78) Wherever there is Lord Krishna, Lord of Yoga
Wherever there is Arjuna,
The mighty bowman
There shall certainly be present,
Victory, opulence extra ordinary power, and righteousness
This is my conclusion.

KRISHNA LEELA

THE DIVINE PASTTIMES OF LORD KRISHNA

DAY ONE

BHUMI MEETS LORD BRAHMA

Bhumi (crying;) – My dear lord, I am so oppressed by the sins on the earth. My heart is heavy and I am carrying a great burden. The demons led by Kamsa Raja have devastated the planet with their sins, persecuting, destroying holy places, capturing and putting in prison pious kings of the earth. They oppress the people with high taxes and injustice.

Lord Brahma – My dear Bhumi, I have been withnessing the great calamity on earth, but somehow we must seek the help of the supreme Lord Vishnu. I am sure He will bring back peace and justice and Dharma on earth. Have patience, Lord Shiva and I and the devatas will go to the ocean of milk to invoke the Supreme Lord.

The devatas recite the Purusha Sukta prayer and later the message comes into the heart of Brahma.

Brahma – My dear devotees of the Supreme. Into my heart has come the message of Vishnu. He, the supreme Lord, will come in person along with His many powers and associates. You must also take birth in Brindavan Mathura in order to help execute His divine will. He will come as the son of Devaki and Vasudeva. Lord Sesa will also accompany him. As well, His external energy in the form of Maya and Durga will appear.

KAMSA MAKES AN ALLIANCE WITH JARASANDHA AFTER A WRESTLING MATCH.

Jarasandha – My dear Kamsa, you have defeated me in wrestling and you are only seven years old. You will be a great king. I therefore present my daughters in marriage to you in order to consolidate a great alliance between our families. In this way we can defeat the devatas favoured by Lord Vishnu.

Kamsa – My dear king Jarasandha, you are my friend today. You are rich and powerful. All the devatas would now be trembling in their boots, knowing that our two families now can rule the world. (To his soldiers) Go after the kings of the Yadu dynasty. They are worshippers of Lord Vishnu. Fight and overpower them and persecute the sadhus, destroy their holy places and kill the cows.

MARRIAGE OF DEVAKI AND VASUDEVA

Kamsa (soliloquy) – My little sister is beautiful. She must have a rich husband. I shall also increase my power and influence by this means. I hear Vasudeva, the son of Surasena, is a handsome youth. Dear priests, arrange for this marriage with haste. It will be the most lavish celebration in the entire world. My power and influence will be known everywhere.

AFTER THE MARRIAGE

Voice from heaven (with thunder preceding) – Kamsa! You are such a fool. You are driving the chariot of your sister. Little do you know that the eighth child of this sister will kill you!

Kamsa (after falling to the ground, stunned by the voice from heaven) – This will never be. No child shall be born. I shall destroy Devaki with my sword. She must die immediately.

Vasudeva – My dear Brother-in-law, you are the greatest, most famous king of the Bhoja dynasty. How come you want to slay your own sister at this most auspicious time of her marriage?

Kamsa – She is my enemy. She must die.

Vasudeva – You are educated, dear brother-in-law. Every moment after birth we are dying. Death is unavoidable. Why should you be so much afraid of death? You as elder brother should protect your sister.

Kamsa – No, no. She must die. I can't be frustrated in my purpose to rule the world.

Vasudeva – My dear Kamsa, the voice in heaven said it is the eight child. Devaki is no threat now. I promise, I will bring the entire children one after the other as they are born for u to do as you please.

Kamsa – Intelligent Brother-in-law, you have today saved me from a great loss of fame. I did not make amistake to choose you as my sister's husband. But I know you will keep your word to bring all the children to me.

NARADA INTERVENES AFTER KAMSA DID NOT KILL THE FIRST BABY

Kamsa – My learned master Narada, welcome. What brings you here?

Naranda – Dear Kamsa, do you know that many devatas are being born in the family of the Yadus. Please look at these marks on the ground. Count from one side. Now count from the other side. The first child of Devaki could be the eight too. You are wise. You can make up your own mind.

Kamsa – O! What a fool I am. Bring Devaki and Vasudeva and the child and I will destroy the child.

Devaki – Dear brother, what can this little child do to you. It is my first. Have mercy.

Kamsa – Luckily, Narada gave me the intelligence. I must kill this child and all others of Devaki's children. Guards! Imprison Devaki and Vasudeva immediately.

LORD VISHNU APPEARS IN THE DARK OF NIGHT IN THE PRISON OF MATHURA. (A great light appears.)

Vasudeva – Behold, O Devaki. The Lord Vishnu himself with chakra, Gada and Padoom. (Both how down before Vishnu)

Devaki – My dear Lord, please make yourself into an ordinary small child. You are the controller of all controllers. Save me from the hands of Kamsa.

Krishna – My dear mother, you are very fortunate. You were very pious in the time of Swayambhu Muni and did great service to Lord Brahma. I appeared to you personally and you requested that I become your beloved child. Do not be afraid. Kamsa will not harm you. I have come to destroy him. (To Vasudeva) Please father, take me to the house of Nanda and Yashoda and the exchange the baby Yashoda for myself. Kamsa cannot destroy the daughter of Yashoda. The daughter child is Yoga Maya herself – Durga Mata.

YOGA-MAYA CONFOUNDS THE PURPOSE OF KAMSA

Soldier – Maharaja, the eighth child of Devaki is born. I can hear the baby crying.

Kamsa – The child must certainly die. Double the guards and bring the child to me.

AFTER THE CHILD IS BROUGHT

Devaki – O my brother, be not so cruel. What can this baby do to you? You have defeated many men and devatas. Please save my child.

Kamsa – No my sister. This child must die. The voice in heaven said it will be my murderer.

KAMSA TRIES TO KILL THE CHILD

Yoga-Maya (Durga) – You rascal! How can you kill me? Your enemy is already born somewhere in the world. Don't be so cruel to your poor sister.

Kamsa – Alas, the gods have defeated me. Dear Devaki and Vasudeva, please forgive me. I have given you great trouble. I have killed my nephews for nothing. The gods themselves, as you can see, make false propaganda. The eighth child could not kill me.

You are free to go your way. I hope you can forgive me.

DAY TWO

DISPLAY OF CHARACTERS AND PARADE AROUND GROUNDS, WITH MUSIC

Scene 1

KAMSA EXPLAINS EVENTS OF PREVIOUS NIGHT IN WHICH DURGA WENT UP IN THE SKY AND TOLD HIM HIS ENEMY IS STILL AT LARGE. KAMSA ASKS COUNCILLORS FOR ADVICE.

First Councillor – Maharaja, Let us make arrangements to kill all children born within the last ten days.

Second Councillor – The devatas will not interfere with us because they fear you have beaten them many times. We are ready to obey your every command.

Third Councillor. My lord Kamsa, let us also destroy the Brahmins and cows, as they are responsible for nourishing the devatas with milk and butter. Please give us your permission. We are eager to carry out your service.

KAMSA GIVES ORDERS TO DESTROY SADHUS, CHILDREN AND COWS.

Scene II

NANDA AND VASUDEVA MEET

Vasudeva – Greetings Nanda Raja, please tell me: is all well with your family? Tell me about your two boys. Kamsa is causing havoc everywhere killing innocent children.

Nanda Raja – My dear King Vasudeva. The Lord has brought me good fortune. My two boys are like jewels. I am favoured by God.

Vasudeva – My dear Nanda, please return to your home if you have already paid you taxes. I forsee some disturbances in Gokula.

Scene III

PUTANA TRIES TO KILL KRISHNA

First Councillor – Maharaja. Why don't you send for the terrible Putana?

Kamsa – Good idea. Go and fetch her.

Putana – What can I do to serve my great Lord? You look all disturbed. What is the matter?

Kamsa – O Putana, my beloved sister, the devatas have baffled me. My enemy is alive. Certainly with your great skill you can find him and destroy him.

Putana – My Lord Maharaja. Please have no worry. I will accomplish my mission.

Scene IV

PUTANA ENTERS GOKULA

First Gopi – Look at that beautiful lady. She looks like Laksmi, the goddness of fortune. She is so charming.

Second Gopi – Come, my sisters. Let's follow her.

PUTANA ENTERS THE HOUSE OF MOTHER YASHODA

Putana – Sister Yashoda, what a beautiful son you have. Could I play with him for a while?

Yashoda – Certainly you can play with my little boy.

Scene V

Yashoda – Kanhaiya, Kanhaiya, where are you my little one? Where is that lady who took my child? I suspect some great calamity.

Gopi – Come Mother Yashoda. Let's find our dear Krishna.

Yashoda – Pyare beta Kahaiya. Did that great demon harm you in any way? Oh, it is only by the grace of Lord Vishnu that you are saved.

TRINAVARTA IS DESTROYED (Sound of a great wind)

VASUDEVA SENDS GARGA MUNI TO THE HOUSE OF NANDA RAJA

Vasudeva – My dear Guru, please go to the house of Nanda Raja across the Jamuna to conduct the ceremonies for purification and calculate the future of Krishna by your skill as an astrologer.

NAME GIVING CEREMONY OF KRISHNA AND BALARAMA AND THE VISION OF VISHVARUPA

Scene I

Nanda Maharaja – My dear Brahmana, welcome to my home. Your appearance in homes is to enlighten the householders. We are always engaged in household duties and we forget our real duty to find out about our souls and how to get back to God. Your coming here is to enlighten us about spiritual life.

THE NARRATOR SPEAKS ABOUT THE QUALITIES OF BRAHMINS AND GARGA MUNI, FAMOUS ASTROLOGER. (jyotishi)

Garga Muni – My dear Nanda, Vasudeva has sent me to see to the purification rituals of these boys. It seems to me that Krishna is the son of Vasudeva. To do a big ceremony would attract the soldiers of Kamsa.

Nanda – since there is such danger, then we will secretly hold the ceremony in a cowshed.

Garga Muni – The elder son of mother Rohini will be called Balrama, He will be very strong. He will also be called Sankarshana. As far as the other boy is concerned, this little boy has taken a different complexion in different yugas (ages). First white, then red, yellow and now dark blue or black. Some will call him Krishna. Others will call him Vasudeva. Your child, Nanda Raja, is as powerful as Narayana himself. He is so powerful that anyone who becomes his devotee will always be protected and not troubled by enemies.

Scene II

CHATURBHUJ ROOP

Balaram - Mataji, Krishna has been naughty. He has been eating dirt. We all saw him.

Yashoda – My dear Krishna, why have you eaten dirt?

Krishna – No mother! My brother Balaram and my friends have ganged up on me. They are speaking lies. I did not eat clay. My brother Balarama, while playing with me, got angry and so he decided to complain against me. If you think they are telling the truth then you can look inside my mouth to see if there is any clay.

Yashoda – All right, my son. If you have not eaten any clay then just open your mouth so I can see.

YASHODA SEES THE UNIVERSAL FORM OF GOD – VISHVA RUPA – OUTER SPACE, SUN, MOON, STARS ALL THE DEVATAS, BRAHMA, SHIVA, VISHNU – ETERNAL TIME – ALSO KRISHNA ON HER LAP.

Yashoda – This is the cosmic, mystic power of my child. Let e bow down to God and worship Him.

GOPIES COMPLAIN TO YASHODA MATA

First Gopi – Dear mother Yashoda, your two boys are stealing our dahi and butter and breaking our pots in the dark, dark rooms.

Third Gopi – These two boys Krishna and Balarama exhibit a glow in their bodies that allows them to see in the dark.

Fourth Gopi – They steal our ghee and dahi. We cannot punish them. They are so charming. They smile so sweetly. See how they are smiling at us.

Yashoda – My dear Gopis, I doubt my boys are stealing your butter, but please hide your pots ad lock the doors tightly.

THE FRUIT VENDOR'S FRUIT TURN INTO GOLD.

Vendor – Fruits, fruits for sale. Beautiful fruits. What a beautiful child. Look at His eyes.

His beautiful blue colour, His enchanting smile. He is like an angel.

MOTHER YASHODA CALLS KRISHNA HOME, BUT HE IS TOO BUSY PLAYING.

Yashoda – Kanhaiya! My Kanhaiya! Where are you my son? Please come home. You think you are a street boy, that you have no home. Today is your birthday. You should give charity to the Brahmins. Come, change your dress, then you can go and play again.

NANDA'S BROTHER, UPANANDA, ADVISES NANDA TO LEAVE GOKULA FOR BRINDABAN.

BAKASURA ATTACKS KRISHNA ON THE BANK OF THE YAMUNA

Balarama – Dear Krishna, see what a formidable Demon Bird. Its beak looks strong as a thunderbolt and it looks fierce. It is going to attack.

BAKASURA TRIED TO PINCH KRISHNA WITH HIS BEAK. THEN HE TRIED TO SWALLOW KRISHNA, BUT THERE WAS FIRE IN HIS THROAT AND HE COULD NOT DO SO. THEN KRISHNA SPLIT THE BEAK OF THE DEAMON LIKE SOME ONE SPLITS A BLADE OF GRASS.

Gwala Bala – Oh, how strong is Krishna. He breaks the jaws of the demon. He splits the beak as easily as one splits a blade of grass.

BALARAMA AND KRISHNA ACT AS RAMA AND LAKSMANA AND THEIR FRIENDS LIKE MONKEYS CONSTRUCTING A BRIDGE.

AGHASURA IS KILLED.

KRISHNA, BALARAMA AND THEIR FRIENDS FOLLOW THE MONKEY ON THE TREES. THEN AFTER PLAY THEY SIT DOWN TO LUNCH. AGHASURA EXPANDS HIMSELF BY HIS YOGIC POWER, MAHIMA SIDDHI, TO EIGHT MILES. HIS MOUTH IS LIKE A MOUNTAIN CAVE.

First Gwala Bala – This animal's upper lip is just like the sunshine. Second Gwala Bala – His mouth looks like a mountain cave. That long highway is its tongue.

Third Gwala Bala – Inside, its mouth is dark blue like in a mountain cave.

Fourth Gwala Bala – This demon would swallow all of us, but certainly he cannot swallow Krishna. Krishna is capable of killing the demon as he did Bakasura.

KRISHNA ENTERS THE DEMON AFTER HIS FRIENDS.

Devatas – Alas! Alas!

Kamsa – Ha! Ha! Ha! Ha1 Let's see if Krishna could survive our friend Aghasura. He is all swallowed up. He is dead. He is dead

Lord Krishna expands Himself, exploding the demon head, thus saving all his friends

Devatas – Jai Jai Krishna! Jai Hari! Jai Hari!

STEALING OF THE BOYS and CALVES BY BRAHMA

Krishna – My dear friends. See what a pretty spot this is, for taking lunch and playing on the soft sandy bank of the Jamuna. You can see the open lotus flowere so beautiful, giving off a sweet smell. The birds are singing, and the peacocks are calling, and there is echoing of the sounds of the animals. Let us have lunch here. It is late and we are hungry. While we lunch the calves can enjoy the soft grass.

First Gwala Bala – Krishna! Krishna! The cows are entering the deep forest. Krishna!

Second Gwala Bala – Krishna! Krishna is the personified killer of fear. Krishna will help us.

Krishna – My dear friends. Do not interrupt your lunch. I will see to the calves.

BRAHMA STEALS THE COWS

Brahma – There is little Krishna who, I am told, just destroyed the huge snake demon Aghasura. The noise of his death made a great sound reaching up into the heavens.

Is this little boy really myLlord and Master? I will soon find out.

BRAHMA THEN HIDES THE BOYS AND CALVES IN A CAVE.

Krishna – Lord Brahma has stolen my friends and the calves. I cannot return alone to Brindavan. It would break the hearts of the mothers of the children and the hearts of the mother cows. I can find these cows nowhere here. I will expand myself by my own yoga-maya and produce exact copies of these boys and calves. No one will know the difference.

BRAHMA MARVELS AT THE POWER OF KRISHNA AND SURRENDERS TO HIM.

Brahma – All the boys and calves are asleep in the cave but here I can see all of them before Krishna. My mystic power! Does it have no influence over these boys and calves. I am confused. My mystic power seems useless here.

THE BOYS AND CALVES SUDDENLY BECOME VISHNU FORMS WITH BRAHMAS, SHIVAS AND OTHER DEVATAS AND OTHER SMALLER CREATURES DANCING AROUND THE VISHNU FORMS.

Brahma – What a wonderful, perplexing sight. My power is limited. There are many other Brahmas and Sivas as I could see. Lord Vishnu is the supreme master and we are all his servants.

QUOTE – NIBODH TATEDAM ...

BRAHMA SURRENDERS TO KRISHNA AND OFFERS PRAYERS.

Brahma – My dear Lord. Please excuse me for disturbing you in your Leela with your friends and calves. I bow down to you again and again. Grant me your mercy. You are the Supreme God. Infallible. You are Mukunda, the giver of liberation. You are the one supreme Lord without a second. You have expamded yourself as Vishnu, as Lord Shiva the destroyer and myself as creator. But you are the true creator, maintainer and destroyer. You incarnate as Rama, as Parashurama, as Vamana deva (the dwarf), as Narasimha (the man-lion), as Varaha (the boar) and as Matsya (the fish). You protect the devotees and destroy the demons. You have proved that you are the supreme controller and we are your servants. Let me go please. Forgive me.

DAY THREE

First Gopi – Dear friends, Our Vrindavanna forest is proclaiming the glories of the entire earth because this planet is glorified by the lotus foot prints of the son of Devaki. Resides, when Govinda plays the flute the peacocks immediately become mad. When the trees and plants on Govardhana hill see the dancing of the peacocks they stand still and listen to the transcendental sound of the flute with great attention.

Second Gopi – My deal friends, just see the deer. They are dumb animals. Not only are they attracted by the dress of

Krishna and Balarama, but they all bow down to Krishna when they hear the flute.

Third Gopi – The cows are also charmed by the music. They spread and raise their ears to the nectar of his music.

STEALING OF TH CARMENTS OF THE UNMARRIED GOPIS

Gopis – O Mother Durga, O Katyayani, O Supreme Eternal Energy of God. Please be kind to me and arrange for my marriage with the son of Maharaja Nanda.

Krishna – Dear girls. Please come here one after another and pray for your garments and then take them away. I am not joking. I am telling you the truth. I know you have worshipped goddess Durga. So please come out. I want to see your complete beauty.

Gopis – You are the son of Maharaja Nanda. Please deliver our garments or we will complain to Nanda Maharaja and Raja Kamsa. We are your servants, but we cannot do this.

Krishna – My dear girls, if you think you are my eternal servitors and always willing to do what I say then come close one after another.

(Narrator explains that a devotee must renounce al lattchment in orde rto surrender to God supreme)

DELIVERING THE WIVES OF THE BRAHMANS

Gwala –Dear Krishna and Balarama you are all powerful. You kill demons. But we are hungry. Please arrange for getting us food.

Krishna – My dear friends, please go to the house of the Brahmans. They are doing sacrifices to go to the heavenly planets. These Brahamans are not worshippers of Vishnu. They are chanting the Vedic hymns though they do not know that the purpose of the Vedas is to know Me.

Boys – Lord Vishnu, as Krishna and Balarama are nearby and request food, please give some food to us.

The brahmans refuse.

Boys (speaking to the wives of the Brahmans) – Dear Mothers, please accept our obeisances. Lord Krishna and Balarama are nearby. They have sent us here. We are hungry, therefore give us some food, please.

THE WIVES GO TO KRISHNA AND BALARAMA

Krishna – My dear wives of the Brahmans. Welcome. You are fortunate. You have ignored the protests of your husbands, brothers and fathers in order to see me. This is completely right. Doing Bhakti to me without wanting anything for your personal self is the best thing for all living beings. Now you must go back to your husbands As my devotees your husbands will take you back and, in fact, all people and the devatas will be satisfied with you.

WORSHIP OF GOVARDHANA HILL

Krishna – My dear father, what are these arrangements for a sacrifice all about? What is the result and for whom is it meant?

Nanda – We are doing sacrifice to Indra because he has given us rains. It is because of his mercy that we get rain.

Krishna – My dear father. I do not think you have to worship any devata to get help for your agriculture. See the rain falls also in the sea. You do not have to worship Indra. Our duty is to protect cows. Our special relationship is with Govardhana Hill. So, now let us make a sacrifice to Govardhana Hill and not to Indra. I am Govardhana Hill, as you will see.

INDRA SHOWERS HEAVY RAINS ON BRINDAVAN

Indra – By neglecting to sacrifice to the devatas and me the inhabitants of Brindavan must pay dearly. They have listened to the talkative boy named Krishna. He is nothing but a child. By listening to him they have enraged me. I will flood their village with ceaseless, heavy rain night and day.

Inhabitants – O Govinda, O Krishna. You are all powerful. Please save us.

Krishna – This devata (archangel) thinks he is supreme. I will take away his false prestige. The devatas are my devotees and therefore this Indra is certainly puffed up with his power. He will be taught a lesson. I will save my devotees by my mystic power.

AFTER KRISHNA HOLDS UP GOVARDHANA HILL WITH HIS LITTLE FINGER

Indra – What a wonder! This little Krishna is the supreme God. I have been wrong, puffed up with my own importance. Please my servants, stop the rain and the thunder the winds and cold immediately.

Heavenly beings– Jai Krishna jai. Jai Hari. Hari jai jai.

Boys – Oh what a wonder! Krishna has lifted Govardhana Hill like a loutus flower and put it down again. Maharaj Nanda, your boy is a genius. He must be a devata.

Nanda – I can only tell you what Garg Muni told me. This boy has appeared many times before. White, red, yellow and now blue. He will be great and protect his devotees.

INDRA SURRENDERS UNTO KRISHNA

Indra – My dear Lord. I was puffed up by my own false prestige. I though you did me wrong but not allowing the farmers to do Indra Yagna. I was wrong. Now I can understand, by your grace, that you are supreme God, transcendental to all material qualities and the supreme king. My Lord, I committed a great offense at your lotus feet because I did not know your unlimited power. I bow down to you and worship you again and again.

Krishna – My dear Indra, I stopped your sacrifice to show you my mercy and revive your memory that I can supreme above all dependent angels and controllers. You can leave now. I forgive you.

THE RASA DANCE

MY DEAR FRIENDS, IF YOU DESIRE TO ENJOY THE COMPANY OF MATERIAL SOCIETY, FRIENDSHIP AND LOVE, THEN PLEASE DO NOT GO TO SEE THE SMILING BOY GOVINDA WHO IS STANDING ON THE BANK OF THE JAMUNA AND PLAYING HIS FLUTE. HIS LIPS ARE BRIGHTENED BY THE BEAMS OF THE FULL MOONLIGHT.

First Gopi – Husband! Father! Do not restrain me! I must go to see my Govinda

Second Gopi – Since I am locked in my room then I will meditate on my Shyamsundara.

I will dance with Him in my heart as the yogis see Him clearly in their hearts.

Gopis (after Krishna says they should go home) – O Govinda! We are all surrendered souls. Please accept us. Dance with us. Do not be so cruel. We have left everything behind just to follow you.

RASA DANCE

Krishna – O damsels, O Ladies of Vrindavana, you are very fortunate and very dear to me. I am pleased that you have come to me. I hope all is well in Vrindavana. Now please what can I do for you. Why have you come here knowing that there are ferocious animals – tigers, bears, wolves – in the forest. Please return immediately. A woman must be faithful to her husband and take care of the children, so please return. Even if your husband is not rich, or if he is sick, or paralysed or not of good character you should not leave him. So please go home.

Krishna (after gopis dance with him) – The gopis have become proud at their fortune of dancing with me. I will show them my mercy by curbing their pride. I will disappear from them.

AFTER KRISHNA SPEAKS

Third Gopi – Dear Krishna, We can no longer engage our hearts in family affairs. We have developed a different type of love which is continually blazing in our hearts.

Fourth Gopi – Dear Krishna, you are known as Hari. You destroy all miseries of all living beings. You are their eernal friend, especially those who have left everything and surrendered their lives to you.

Fifth Gopi – Dear Govinda, we are captivated by seeing you with tilaka and earrings, by seeing your beautiful face and your enchanting smile. Your vibrating flute melts our hearts.

AKURA INSTRUCTED BY KAMSA

Kamsa – My dear Akrura, I have no better friend than you in the Yadu and Bhoja Dynasty. Actually, I am begging you. Please go to Vrindavana and find the two boys Krishna and Balarama. They are sons of Nanda Maharaja. Take this good chariot.

(Kamsa, speaking to supporters) Now my plan is to kill the two boys. The elephant Kuvalyapida will probably kill them. If they escape, the wrestlers will kill them. I will also kill Vasudeva and Nanda and also Ugrasena and Devaki. With Jarasandha's help I will kill all the kings on the earth because these kings support Dharma and Vishnu.

Akrura – My king, your plan sounds good. But your plans may not be successful. Man proposes, but God disposes. If your plan are not sanctioned by God they will fail. I shall bring Krishna and Balarama here, as you want. The supreme Lord had now come as an ordinary human being and I will be able to see Him face to face. I will see those lotus feet which are worshipped by Brahma, Shiva and Narada.

K rishna – My dear Akrura. What shall I enquire of you. I know you are protected by Kamsa who is cruel and demonic. Kamsa is so sinful he killed the sons of his sister who should have been protected by him.

AKRURA EXPLAINS THAT KAMSA WANTS TO KILL VASUDEVA ETC.

Gopis (crying) – O Providence, you are cruel. Krishna is cruel too. He is leaving us although we are surrendered to him. Akrura is mean. He is taking away our Shyamsundar.

GOSPEL OF PERFECTION (BHAGWAT GITA)

Dr. Roopnarine Singh, devotee of Lord Krishna and the Bhagwat Gita, since youth, is a distinguished exponent of Sanatan Dharma, the religion of the Hindus.

He has created 16 Krishna and Ram Leelas in Trinidad(11), Montreal, (5) and Toronto (1).

He is a cardiologist, educated at Mc Gill University, but he has become the doctor of the heart of love, and selfless devotion to God Supreme – Lord Krishna and the Gita. His Career is distinguished by excellence and Virtue and Service to Mankind and the the Gospel of Perfection – a new name for the Bhagwat Gita,18 chapters and 701 verses, in a colour book. The Gospel of Perfection in discipline, duty, knowledge and pure love, is the formula to attain peace, happiness, prosperity and nobility, by serving

GOD SUPREME, the embodiment of PURE LOVE (U-LOVE),

Unconditional, Unselfish and Universal Love, and everyone is eligible to taste the divine waters of His grace, love and precious beauty, power and greatness. **Free on internet at hinduroyalsociety.com**

DO NOT HURRY, DO NOT WORRY, DO NOT BE SORRY.

DO YOUR WORK AND DUTY PERFECTLY.

FIND THE LORD OF GLORY IN YOUR HEART, AND BY HIS LIGHT,

FIND PEACE HAPPINESS, PROSPERITY AND NOBILITY AND GREATNESS.

This is the message of the Bhagvat Gita

LORD KRISHNA AND ARJUNA

IN BHAGWAT GITA

Dr. Roopnarine Singh

Bsc.Hons, M.D.CM. (McGill), C.S.P.Q (Quebec)FRCPC

Founder Roopnarine Singh Bsc. Hons. M.D.CM. (McGILL),

C.S.P.Q (Quebec) Certified Cardiologist. 1974.

Internet Hindu University Who am I?

My name is Roopnarine Singh, a medical doctor, Cardiologist, in Montreal Canada. I was educated at McGill University and has been living here for thirty seven years. I am a Hindu and has organised sixteen times the Krisna Leela in Montreal, Toronto and Trinidad, West Indies. I have also organised the Canada Day Parade in Montreal for the last 28 years to which over 100,000 people attend each year. I am also an author of a book entitled, Canada, the greatest Nation of the 21st century. This was published in English and French in 1993. In that year also I received the Citation for Citizenship and was decorated by the Government of Canada, one of 25 Canadians honoured that year. My present aim is to create an Internet Hindu university from which Hindus around the world and people seeking enlightment can get definite Knowledge about the Glory, Beauty, Wonder and Super excellence of God and the lofty principles of the Hindu

Religion, and the Fundamental Religion of Sefless Love, Duty, and Holiness. This University will be part of the activities of the ROYAL HINDU SOCIETY OF RAMA AND KRISHNA, which is being organised at present. This idea will be presented in the first paper presented at Concordia University at the instance of the World Diaspora Meeting of Hindus in August 1997, and this will be the first installment to appear in this site.

I recently created from the original Sanskrit, a new version of the glorious Bhagwat Gita, favourite book of Mahatma Gandhi, and Robert Oppenhermir, creater of the first atomic bomb in Nevada. It consist of 701 verses and eighteen chapters in modern scientific and practical English verse form. It has a unique point of view and presents a simple practical scientific and definitely realizable pathway to truth peace, happiness, nobility, greatness and prosperity by the Gospel of Perfection in discipline, duty, knowledge and devotion, culminating in pure love.(Para Bhakti), unconditional, unselfish, and universal love, the nature of God Supreme himself. This love is called U – LOVE. This book is called the Gospel of Perfection.

Printed in the United States
By Bookmasters